THE EFFECTIVE
BOARD OF TRUSTEES

Richard P. Chait
Thomas P. Holland
Barbara E. Taylor

Sponsored by the
CENTER FOR HIGHER EDUCATION GOVERNANCE AND LEADERSHIP

AMERICAN COUNCIL ON
EDUCATION

MACMILLAN
PUBLISHING COMPANY

NEW YORK

Maxwell Macmillan Canada

TORONTO

Maxwell Macmillan International

New York   Oxford   Singapore   Sydney

Macmillan Publishing Company
866 Third Avenue, New York, N.Y. 10022

Maxwell Macmillan Canada, Inc.
1200 Eglinton Avenue East, Suite 200
Don Mills, Ontario M3C 3N1

Macmillan, Inc. is part of the Maxwell
Communication Group of Companies.

The project presented or reported herein was performed
pursuant to grants from the Lilly Endownment, Inc., and
the Office of Educational Research and
Improvement/United States Department of Education
(OERI/ED). However, the opinions expressed herein
do not necessarily reflect the position or policy of the
Lilly Endowment or of OERI/ED, and no official endorsement by
either organization should be inferred.

A project of the Center for Higher Education
Governance and Leadership, the University of Maryland,
College Park.

Library of Congress Catalog Card Number: 91-220

Printed in the United States of America

printing number
 2 3 4 5 6 7 8 9 10

Library of Congress Cataloging-in-Publication Data

Chait, Richard.
    The effective board of trustees.
        p.   cm.—(American Council on Education/Macmillan series on
    higher education)
        "Sponsored by the Center for Higher Education Governance and Leadership."
        Includes bibliographical references and index.
        ISBN 0-02-897088-8
        1. College trustees—United States—Evaluation. 2. Universities
    and colleges—United States—Administration. I. Holland, Thomas P.
    II. Taylor, Barbara E. III. American Council on Education.
    IV. Center for Higher Education Governance and Leadership (U.S.)
    V. Series: American Council on Education/Macmillan series in higher
    education.
    LB2342.5.C43   1991
    378.1'12—dc20   91-220
                                                                       CIP

Contents

Acknowledgments   iv

Introduction   1

1 THE CONTEXTUAL DIMENSION   9

2 THE EDUCATIONAL DIMENSION   26

3 THE INTERPERSONAL DIMENSION   42

4 THE ANALYTICAL DIMENSION   59

5 THE POLITICAL DIMENSION   77

6 THE STRATEGIC DIMENSION   95

7 WHAT'S A PRESIDENT TO DO?   114

References   133

Index   138

Acknowledgments

No one has done more to foster the study of trusteeship than Robert W. Lynn during his tenure as senior vice president at the Lilly Endowment, Inc. We were fortunate to be among the many scholars and practitioners whose interest in governance was nurtured by Bob's intellectual stimulation, moral support, and, through the Endowment, timely grants. We are deeply indebted to Bob and to the Lilly Endowment, Inc.

Support for this study was also provided by a grant from the U.S. Department of Education, Office of Educational Research and Instruction, to the National Center for Postsecondary Governance and Finance at the University of Maryland, where this project was based.

During the early stages of our work, we benefited from the practical and clearheaded counsel of the project's Technical Advisory Committee. Its members included John Aram, Nancy Axelrod, Robert Birnbaum, William Dees, Joseph Kauffman, Robert Mueller, and Blenda Wilson. We also profited from the work done by colleagues at the Association of Governing Boards of Universities and Colleges (AGB) and at the Cheswick Center to raise the sights of trustees and presidents about the contributions capable boards can make to their institutions.

Later in the project, John Aram, Richard Boyatzis, Karen Grochau, and David Kolb, all at Case Western Reserve University, were instrumental in helping us to revise and improve our self-assessment questionnaire for trustees. Throughout the project, we were ably assisted by Lori Potts-Dupre and Joan Lippincott, both graduate students at the University of Maryland. Lori helped us review the pertinent literature and Joan coordinated all the logistics associated with administering the trustee self-assessment. At the same time, Kay Giannuzzi ensured that the clerical aspects of our work proceeded smoc hly day-to-day. As the current phase of our research drew to a close, we received many useful suggestions about where to head next from our colleagues in the National Seminar on Trusteeship, also funded by the Lilly Endowment.

In a study of this sort, which involved extensive site visits and interviews, we owe a special debt to the eighty-six trustees and the twenty-two college presidents who unselfishly carved out the time to talk with us and then spoke so candidly to us about their experiences governing an academic institution. Without their willingness to converse with us, quite simply, this study would not have been possible.

Finally, we would each, in our own way, like to express a special note of gratitude to our spouses—Diane Chait, Martha Cook, and David Johnson—for encouraging us in our efforts, for tolerating our travel schedules, and for abiding those faraway looks that meant we were preoccupied (again) with the study of trusteeship.

Introduction

This book is for trustees and about trustees. It is also in a real sense a book *by* trustees, as it based on the experiences of 108 board members and presidents whom we interviewed at twenty-two independent liberal arts and comprehensive colleges.

Focus of the Book. We started this project with three deceptively simple questions in mind:

1. What characteristics define and describe effective boards of trustees of independent colleges?

2. Do the behaviors of effective and ineffective boards differ systematically?

3. What is the relationship, if any, between board effectiveness and institutional performance?

After three years of research, we arrived at some answers to these questions that, we believe, will be useful to trustees and presidents of independent colleges as well as many other not-for-profit organizations.

Major Findings. This study reached three conclusions that are especially significant for board members and CEOs. We will summarize each major finding and then describe briefly the distinctive aspects of the study's scope and design.

First, and most important, we found that *there are specific characteris-*

tics and behaviors that distinguish strong boards from weak boards. We classified these differences into six distinct dimensions of effective trusteeship that enabled a board as a group to perform effectively. To each of these six dimensions we devote an entire chapter. However, to provide the reader with an overview, exhibit I outlines the essence of each competence.

Second, we ascertained that *there is a positive and systematic association between the board's performance, as measured against these competencies, and the college's performance, as measured against some conventional financial indicators.* We do not assert a causal relationship. In other words, we do not mean to suggest, for example, that college boards of trustees *cause* increases in total operating revenues or institutional wealth. Rather, we discovered that there was a strong congruence between the competencies of effective boards and these institutional performance indicators.

Third, and comparatively less important, we learned that *self-assessments by boards of trustees are of questionable validity as accurate and objective measures of actual board performance and competence.* Perhaps some alternative approaches will overcome the limitations to self-evaluation that we and other researchers have encountered. In the meantime, though, self-studies are likely to be more valuable as springboards to discussion and as measures of self-perception than as reliable barometers of a board's effectiveness.

EXHIBIT I   The Competencies of Governing Boards

I. *Contextual Dimension.* The board understands and takes into account the culture and norms of the organization it governs. The board:

—Adapts to the distinctive characteristics and culture of the college's environment.

—Relies on the institution's mission, values, and traditions as a guide for decisions.

—Acts so as to exemplify and reinforce the organization's core values.

II. *Educational Dimension.* The board takes the necessary steps to ensure that trustees are well-informed about the institution, the profession, and the board's roles, responsibilities, and performance. The board:

—Consciously creates opportunities for trustee education and development.

—Regularly seeks information and feedback on its own performance.

—Pauses periodically for self-reflection, to diagnose its strengths and limitations, and to examine its mistakes.

III. *Interpersonal Dimension*. The board nurtures the development of trustees *as a group*, attends to the board's *collective* welfare, and fosters a sense of cohesiveness. The board:

—Creates a sense of inclusiveness among trustees.

—Develops group goals and recognizes group achievements.

—Identifies and cultivates leadership within the board.

IV. *Analytical Dimension*. The board recognizes complexities and subtleties in the issues it faces and draws upon multiple perspectives to dissect complex problems and to synthesize appropriate responses. The board:

—Approaches problems from a broad institutional outlook.

—Searches widely for concrete information and actively seeks different viewpoints from multiple constituencies.

—Tolerates ambiguity and recognizes that complex matters rarely yield to perfect solutions.

V. *Political Dimension*. The board accepts as one of its primary responsibilities the need to develop and maintain healthy relationships among key constituencies. The board:

—Respects the integrity of the governance process and the legitimate roles and responsibilities of other stakeholders.

—Consults often and communicates directly with key constituencies.

—Attempts to minimize conflict and win/lose situations.

VI. *Strategic Dimension*. The board helps envision and shape institutional direction and helps ensure a strategic approach to the organization's future. The board:

—Cultivates and concentrates on processes that sharpen institutional priorities.

—Directs its attention to priorities or decisions of strategic or symbolic magnitude to the institution.

—Anticipates potential problems and acts before issues become urgent.

Distinctive Aspects of This Study. The literature on trusteeship abounds with books, articles, and pamphlets on governance and board development. Most of these works, however, are "armchair studies" or prescriptive exhortations by seasoned practitioners (e.g., Houle, 1960; 1989; Nason, 1980; O'Connell, 1985; Zwingle, 1975).

We decided to take a different approach so that we could develop a framework of effective trusteeship that was *systematically and empirically tested*. Thus, we relied heavily on the "critical incident" or "behavioral event" technique (Flanagan, 1954; Klemp and McClelland, 1986). On site visits to twenty-two campuses, we asked trustees and presidents to describe at great length significant events that in their judgment exemplified effective trusteeship on the part of their boards. In this way, we gathered highly detailed, firsthand descriptions of the actual *behaviors* of boards of trustees. And by analyzing these rich and extensive transcripts, we were able to determine the underlying competencies and skills associated with these behaviors.

We also decided to focus on the board *as a group* since boards are, in fact, groups. However self-evident that may seem, most previous treatments of governing boards, strangely enough, overlooked group dynamics and group process. Earlier works focused much more on structures, procedures, bylaws, and the "terms and conditions" of trustee appointments, such as length of service, attendance requirements, and committee assignments. In other words, while earlier works examined how the governance game was organized, we concentrated on how it was actually played.

Incidentally, the information that we did gather on structure revealed no systematic patterns of association between board effectiveness and factors such as the board's size, the number and duration of board meetings, and whether there were limits on a trustee's length of service. These data safely allowed only one generalization: large boards wished they were smaller and smaller boards wished they were larger. One board's problem, it seemed, was another board's solution.

The Research Design.[1] In any study of "effectiveness," questions immediately arise about assumptions and definitions (Cameron and Bilimoria, 1985). Since the scholarly trail on "effective" college boards had not been well blazed, we started with a very simple definition: reputation. We asked a handful of acknowledged experts on college trusteeship—authors, consultants, and board mentors—to identify the least and most effective boards that they had encountered *but,* to prevent possible bias on our part, we asked them not disclose to us which boards fit which category. We arranged to visit ten such campuses, where one member of the research team, using the critical incident technique, interviewed for about an hour each the president, the incumbent and immediate past chairperson, and two or three other trustees the board's leaders named as "key trustees."

Each team member independently analyzed each transcript and pinpointed all descriptions of actual board behaviors. Eventually, we refined, sharpened, and combined the behaviors into a set of themes or dimensions that seemed to capture the competencies integral to effective trusteeship, as reflected in the transcripts. We then independently coded and scored every transcript to determine whether and to what degree the various com-

---

[1] For a comprehensive technical report on the research design and on conclusions related to theory and methodology, see T. Holland, R. Chait, and B. Taylor, "Board Effectiveness: Identifying and Measuring Trustee Competencies," *Research in Higher Education*, 30 (4), 451–469.

petencies were manifested. An extremely strong overall consistency emerged among the researchers and also between the researchers and the experts, whose classifications of the boards were now revealed. Based on this phase of the study, we were reasonably confident: (1) that we had identified the essential elements of effective trusteeship; (2) that we could independently reach consistent judgments about a board's competency; and (3) that this approach largely corroborated the experts' judgments.

Next, we wanted to test this tentative framework of board competencies on another sample to determine whether there was any association between board effectiveness and institutional performance. Therefore, we changed the criterion for site selection from expert opinion to a score based on a cluster of commonly applied and readily available institutional performance indicators that included changes in total operating revenues, changes in net student revenues, institutional wealth, financial reserves, and "academic emphasis," a measure of the proportion of institutional funds invested directly in the academic aspects of the enterprise.

Institutions were rank ordered in terms of changes in total revenue patterns between 1981–1982 through 1985–1986, and then their ranks on the other criteria were added. We then selected twelve sites that exhibited the most consistent and extreme sets of scores over the five-year period as follows: two with the steepest uninterrupted proportional *gains*; two with the steepest uninterrupted proportional *declines*; two with the sharpest *upward reversal* of a previous downward pattern; and six with the greatest *absolute* gains. We reiterate that we did not assume or test a causal relationship between board competencies and institutional performance. Instead, the purpose was to determine whether these institutional indicators were *systematically associated* with dimensions of board effectiveness.

We replicated the process that we used in the first phase of the study. Our individual ratings of the critical incident interviews were once again extremely consistent with one another, *and* our overall scores for each site (and for most of the individual competency scores) were, in fact, systematically associated with the institutions' performance indicators. The sites with the strongest board competency scores were the colleges with the greatest proportional gains, followed by schools with the steepest upward reversals and the greatest absolute gains. The sites with the lowest board-competency scores were the colleges with the greatest proportional declines. We then conducted a similar analysis of the first ten sites, and seven of the nine institutions (data were unavailable for one) evidenced consistency between the board's competency scores and the institution's performance indicators.

Unfortunately, however, attempts to measure effectiveness through trustee self-evaluations were not as successful with either the first or second sample of boards, even though we substantially revised the self-study questionnaire between these two phases of the study. (See chapter 2 for a further explanation of the flaws seemingly inherent to self-evaluations.)

Effectiveness Defined. We were able to define and describe "effectiveness" based on *multiple references*: reputation among experts, scores on structured interviews, and institutional performance indicators. Based on these multiple references, we grouped the twenty-two boards into three categories: we classified seven as "effective," seven as "midrange," and eight as "ineffective." In the text we sometimes refer to the three most effective boards as "exemplary" or "extremely effective," and to the three least effective as "extremely ineffective" or "extremely weak."

It is imperative to note that not all of the effective boards had mastered every competency and not all of the ineffective boards were uniformly weak. Obviously, each board was stronger on some dimensions than others. On balance, however, the effective boards exhibited a greater *overall* degree of proficiency and usually had higher scores, relative to the ineffective boards, on each of the competencies.

Nevertheless, board members and presidents should not feel compelled to *excel* in each dimension of effective trusteeship or to institute immediately a series of actions designed to improve the board's performance on each competency simultaneously. Any attempt to do so would probably overload and perhaps overwhelm even quite able boards and presidents. A wiser course of action would be to identify first those areas that most require improvement and then concentrate on actions designed to strengthen the board's effectiveness in that specific dimension of trusteeship. In this regard, we wish to stress that each of the effective approaches and behaviors we describe herein has actually been implemented by one or more of the boards we studied. We believe, therefore, that these practices are eminently feasible and not pie-in-the-sky recommendations.

We should also note that the twenty-two colleges in this study spanned the spectrum from elite institutions to far less selective schools, as measured by acceptance rates and SAT/ACT scores. We did not find that academically prestigious colleges, *ipso facto*, have effective boards; two of the most distinguished institutions in the study had midrange boards. Similarly, three of the seven most effective boards governed colleges that were financially secure, well-positioned within their markets, and clear about their purposes, even though they were not among the nation's most renowned institutions of higher education. We mention this only to dispel any notions that only (and all) eminent colleges have effective boards and that institutions of more modest academic reputations do not.

Organization and Limitations of the Book. Each of the first six chapters covers a different competency, but follows the same format. Each begins with a definition of the specific competency and some of the key board actions or "behavioral indicators" that denote that competency. The second section, which often introduces some central concepts from the literature on group dynamics and organizational behavior, explains, compares, and contrasts some of the most representative and illustrative critical incidents we collected. Here the reader can "listen" to trustees and presidents talk about their board's behaviors and thus observe the differences between effective and ineffective boards. The third segment of each chapter presents suggestions for trustees and presidents who would like to take some practical and, we think, helpful measures to improve their board's performance as regards the particular competency under discussion. Finally, each chapter closes with some discussion questions and exercises that boards might use to be more reflective about their behavior and to open or further dialogue about enhancing their effectiveness.

The last chapter, aimed primarily at presidents, explores the implications of this study for CEOs and recommends some steps they can take to improve their boards' effectiveness. Even though the lion's share of this book specifically addresses board members and board behaviors, we believe that the president and the board must, as Peter Drucker recommended, "work as one team of equals" (1990, p. 10). Each clearly has the capacity to influence the other's performance and effectiveness.

Due to a number of important differences between the governance of private and public institutions, we limited the present study to boards of independent colleges. Public boards are usually not self-perpetuating; many are appointed by elected officials and operate within a partisan political arena. We believe that trustees of public college boards, as a rule, have less consensus than their peers at independent colleges about the board's fundamental role. Whatever their philosophical or educational differences, trustees of private colleges almost invariably perceive the board's essential role as being the guardian of the institution's long-term welfare. We have the impression from news reports and from workshops and conversations with many trustees of public institutions that they, in contrast, often view themselves as public watchdogs, constituency representatives, or emissaries of partisan political interests. In addition, many public boards cannot, as a matter of state statute, meet privately, in whole or in part, or conduct a closed and confidential retreat to reflect freely and to speak bluntly about the board's performance. Others are reluctant, in any case, to invest public funds for this purpose.

While such fundamental differences dictated that we confine this project to independent colleges, our findings may suggest implications for further study of public-sector boards. On the other hand, we believe that the results reported here will be immediately useful and applicable to boards of other self-controlled nonprofit organizations, such as independent hospitals, museums, schools, and social-service agencies.

On the Road to Effective Governance. There are more than 1.25 million nonprofit boards, exclusive of governmental agencies, and more than 48,000 college trustees alone (Houle, 1989, p. 195; AGB, *Composition of*

Governing Boards, 1986, p. 7). Nearly all of these volunteers want to be effective board members, yet most are uncertain about how to do so for several reasons. First, the vast majority of trustees are not systematically prepared for the role prior to their appointment to a governing board. "It's a bit like parenthood," one trustee told us, "one day it just happens, and while you can draw on your experiences to date, nothing in life to that point quite prepares for you for *this* role." Second, not many trustees have the benefit of a thorough orientation or ongoing board-development programs after joining a board. Finally, much of the "knowledge" about trusteeship might better be described as conventional wisdom that has not been empirically based or methodically tested. As a result, trustees and presidents must draw more upon hand-me-down shibboleths than upon a solid body of knowledge about governance and its influence on not-for-profit organizations. Ultimately, therefore, many boards of trustees constitute a collection of "successful" individuals who do not perform well as a group. The parts sum to less than the whole.

Even under the most favorable conditions, colleges and other not-for-profit organizations would want their boards of trustees—the bodies legally responsible and ultimately accountable for their institutions' welfare—to function effectively. "The first lesson to be learned," Drucker advised, "is that nonprofits need a clear and functioning governance structure. They have to take their governance seriously, and they have to work hard on it" (1990, p. 8). Moreover, as we enter an era when nonprofits will almost certainly face keener competition for resources, greater calls for accountability, less stability in the external environment, and a heightened need to steer a strategic course over the long term, the value of an able board will be even more pronounced. We hope this book helps trustees to better meet those important challenges and to more effectively discharge their vital responsibilities.

1

The Contextual Dimension

DEFINITION

Competency 1 concerns the **contextual dimension** of governance: the ability of a board of trustees to understand and take into account the culture and norms of the organization it governs. Effective college boards: (1) adapt to the distinctive characteristics of an academic environment; (2) rely on the institution's mission, values, and traditions as a guide for decisions; and (3) act so as to exemplify and reinforce the organization's core values.

DESCRIPTIONS

In the early 1980s, best-sellers such as *Theory Z* (Ouchi, 1981), *In Search of Excellence* (Peters and Waterman, 1982), and *Corporate Cultures* (Deal and Kennedy, 1982) popularized the concept of organizational culture. Not long thereafter, several studies recognized the importance of organizational culture to the effective leadership of colleges and universities (Dill, 1982; Masland, 1985; Tierney, 1988). Indeed, the notion assumed such significance that Schein (1985, p. 2) hypothesized that the "only thing of real importance that leaders do is to create and manage culture."

Just what is organizational culture? The term has been defined as "a system of informal rules that spells out how people are to behave most of the time" (Deal and Kennedy, 1982, p. 15), as "particular webs of significance within an organizational setting" (Tierney, 1988, p. 4), and as "a pattern of basic assumptions—invented, discovered, or developed by a given group as it learns to cope with its problems of external adaptation and internal integration—that has worked well enough to be considered valid and, therefore, be taught to new members as the correct way to perceive, think, and feel in relation to these problems" (Schein, 1985, p. 9). In sum, culture encompasses the deeply embedded assumptions and heuristics that define and hold an organization together.

The assumptions that comprise the cornerstones of organizational culture are revealed through the institution's value statements, behaviors, stories, legends, heroes, language, ritual, and ceremonies. These interpretive events convey to insiders and outsiders what the organization "means" and what it stands for.

Effective boards clearly heeded Schein's admonition to "give culture its due" (p. 314)—both the culture of the academic profession and the culture of the local institution. They were sensitive to their college's context and they were careful in their actions to exemplify and reinforce key elements of the culture.

1. **Effective boards appreciate and adapt to the distinctive characteristics of an academic environment.**

As most perceptive trustees soon realize, colleges and universities are unusual organizations with many distinctive features. The most important characteristic elements of an academic culture include: (1) ambiguous, multiple, immeasurable, and sometimes contradictory goals; (2) an emphasis on shared governance and collegiality; and (3) an unusual degree of professional autonomy, especially for faculty (Chait, 1979; Baldridge et al., 1978). Moreover, like other segments of the not-for-profit sector, institutions of higher education are not primarily motivated or measured by the "bottom line." Barometers of performance are, therefore, vague and imperfect.

These organizational traits are odd notions to many trustees, especially those from the corporate sector. From a typical trustee's perspective, colleges are in many respects a foreign culture with strange customs and curious business practices. As one trustee admitted, "The coffee-can philosophy of accounting—you put money in little cans for specific purposes—is bewildering. And the lines of authority and discipline are muted, less firm. To anyone in business, to be where someone has tenure is baffling." How trustees react to such alien concepts differs between effective and ineffective boards.

Members of more effective boards acknowledged and adapted to the academy's idiosyncrasies, as respectful tourists might do while overseas. This sensitivity to the indigenous culture was exemplified by two members of a competent board:

In business, I make lots of decisions all the time about money and personnel. I like exercising power, but decisions are made differently in a college. It took me five years to learn this.

Academe is entirely unique. So many people who come on the board think they can treat the college like a business. It takes years, but most finally adapt to the differences. You just can't make command decisions in a college.

If stronger boards were able to acclimate to the academic context, members of ineffective boards were more prone to voice exasperation about campus governance. Frustrated by the faculty's failure to act on his suggestion that the college switch from quarters to semesters, the chairman of an ineffective board complained:

I would not want to be chairman again because of the strange nature of management in the academic world. There is no bottom line, no time frame. It's diabolical when it comes to management. . . . The most frustrating thing is the amount of time it takes to complete anything after having reached consensus. It is always such a slow and devious process, never straightforward or a single factor. No one assumes blame. I am a retired military officer trained in management. I dealt with management on the technical side where there is less need to persuade people about how management should get done. . . . My key concern is accountability. Somewhere, someone has to put up or shut up.

Representative of many trustees on less effective boards, this chairman was not so much blind to the academy's unique culture as unable to adapt. There was little readiness to acclimate to the academy. Indeed, one board member referred to the offices of academic, student, and financial affairs as "staff agencies" within the "bureaucracy" that "interface with the relevant trustee committee." Somewhat like the caricature of the "ugly American" abroad, many members of weaker boards would rather alter the local environment than adapt to it. Thus, less effective boards pressed to inject "sound business practices" into campus governance, and they expected to modify the academic culture so that it approximated more closely their own familiar world and their own prior experiences. These trustees did not heed Schein's admonition that "culture controls the manager more than the manager controls the culture" (p. 314).

The differential capacities of boards to adjust to the academic culture was perhaps most conspicuously revealed in critical incidents about faculty autonomy and academic tenure. A trustee of an effective board, while clearly not enamored with either practice, allowed that:

The old style of benevolent dictator doesn't work for a college like it does for a business. The board has had to learn a new style. . . . We business people have had a hard time swallowing things like tenure. We had to learn how you deal with faculty and college administrators. Things aren't like they used to be or how they are in some parts of the business world, where the senior man can hire and fire at will and everybody else goes along with it.

On the other side of the ledger, we interviewed five key trustees at a college that recently had voted to eliminate tenure as part of a larger revision of faculty personnel policies. Only one trustee even recalled the issue, as if the board's action was not terribly noteworthy. And that one trustee stated:

> We took a lot of power from the faculty and gave it to the administration. It was probably the biggest decision we made since I've been here. . . . The decision caused much discussion; time will tell if we made the right decision. It struck a good chord with the board whose members are largely self-employed.

In other words, the board viewed the decision through the familiar, yet inappropriate, lens of self-employed businessmen. Hence, the board ratified the president's recommendation despite the faculty's strong opposition. "The board took [tenure] by the horns and passed the resolution anyway," a trustee said.

More to the point, the board had selected this candidate to be president several years earlier largely because he was an outspoken opponent of tenure. Scarcely considered was whether such an outspoken opponent of tenure could gain and sustain the faculty's support. The president has since departed. By contrast, when a more effective board started a search for a new president, the trustees "all agreed that we had to have someone who was qualified and experienced academically, who had come up through the faculty ranks, and who had demonstrated administrative skills in an academic organization." This board realized that few college presidents can lead effectively or for long without academic legitimacy and faculty support.

By calling attention to the fact that effective boards were more comfortable with the academic context, we do not mean to suggest that trustees must lie down and surrender or accept categorically all elements and implications of that culture. Rather we believe that better boards were able to "do business" more effectively because they were generally sympathetic to the precepts of the profession, more aware of the expectations and constraints these norms created, and more attuned to the likely consequences of violating any basic tenets. In a word, then, these boards understood the ingredients of "appropriate" behavior and were thus better equipped to decide when and whether to act differently.

2. The actions of effective boards are guided by institutional mission, tradition, and history.

Like other nonprofit organizations, colleges and universities aspire to fulfill certain purposes. As quoted by Peter Drucker, America's management guru, (1989, p. 89), a prominent corporate executive stated, "The businesses I work with start their planning with financial resources. The nonprofits start with the performance of their mission." The overall or superordinate goals of a college are typically embodied in a mission statement that provides guidance and direction to all members of the campus community, from students to trustees. Effective boards understand that mission especially well and rely on it as the essential context for major decisions. Less effective boards do not.

This difference between effective and ineffective boards comes as no surprise. The importance of a clearly defined mission to organizational strategy and success has been extensively recognized and documented (Chaffee, 1984; Keller, 1983). Likewise, the board's singular role as the ultimate architect and guardian of a college's mission has been repeatedly emphasized. In conversations with experienced trustees, Houle (1989, p. 123) concluded that the single most important characteristic of a cohesive board was that "the board members share a clear understanding of and commitment to the mission of the agency." Carver (1990, p. 56) ranked "clarifying and sustaining the organization's mission" as "the most important work of any governing board. . . . It is a perpetual obligation, deserving of the majority of board time and energy. . . . It is far more important than any other board undertaking, including . . . choice of chief executive." Naturally enough, then, the Association of Governing Boards (AGB) labels the very first criterion of its self-study questionnaire for trustees "Institutional Mission and Educational Policy."

In light of the pivotal significance of a well-defined and understood mission, the real surprise appears to be that so many trustees are still unable to articulate their college's mission, especially when one considers that independent liberal-arts colleges, unlike "multiversities," tend be single-purpose institutions. Yet, that is precisely what we discovered on about a third of the campuses we visited when we asked trustees, "What are the hallmark characteristics of this institution, the distinctive aspects that set this college apart from others?"

Members of ineffective boards, almost without exception, struggled to answer the question. Some offered bland, nondescript language about demographic characteristics, for example, "We're small, private, and rural." When encouraged to be more specific, these respondents faltered. On one campus, for instance, responses to follow-up probes included comments such as:

This is a fine place. It provides a good education and preparation for a career.

I don't know. I guess it's much like any other small liberal arts college in this region.

That's a question we're trying to answer for ourselves.

Right now, I think that the deficit is driving the college instead of any shared mission.

Small wonder, then, that a prominent out-of-town businessman on this board observed that "the board is out of control and will continue to be until it comes to terms with reality and establishes a clear direction." We were amazed that on another campus three of four trustees cited the *president* as the institution's most distinctive attribute!

In contrast to such responses, nearly all trustees on exceptional boards offered internally consistent and reasonably detailed portraits of their college's hallmark characteristics and mission. Representative of the respondents on one especially effective board, the current chairman stated:

This college is unique in this state. It is a top-quality, small, private liberal-arts college that provides individualized teaching and stresses excellence in all aspects of scholarship. The curriculum is varied but generally we combine preprofessional studies with a strong liberal arts foundation. Our graduates enjoy a very high rate of acceptance into graduate and professional degree programs at leading universities elsewhere. We do have an athletics program, but it plays a supportive role, not dominating the campus as you see at some places.

Among effective boards there was also more frequent and explicit reference to the college's history and heritage. Trustees conveyed with conviction that the board was entrusted with deeply valued traditions. Personal identification with the college's mission was evidenced by remarks such as: "I just am in love with this college. It has always been a warm, personal part of my life" and "I have had a lifelong love affair with this college."

With respect to mission, the dissimilarity between effective and ineffective boards was not limited merely to affection or eloquence of expression. More importantly, trustees on the most effective boards *routinely* invoked the college's mission and traditions as a touchstone and litmus test for decisions that ranged from physical plant to faculty appointments to curriculum revisions. A few vignettes follow.

On a campus that was about to build a new sports facility, a former board chairman recalled, "We reminded ourselves that the quality of life and health for *all* the students, faculty, and staff was our goal, not just that of the athletes." So the facility, the equipment, and the schedule were designed to ensure "that everyone's needs are met, not just a favored few." In effect, as form follows function, here the mission determined the plan for a new facility.

The president and board of trustees of a college which historically had only appointed Christians to the faculty decided "that it would be good for the college to broaden the diversity, so long as that did not conflict with the basic mission of the college." Not long after, an offer was extended to a non-Christian who subsequently allowed that he could not accept and might attempt to overturn the college's mission as a Christian school. When the offer was therefore withdrawn, some faculty and students accused the college of discrimination. At the suggestion of the board chairman, the president and board held several open meetings to explain that "we had not refused this man a position due to his religion, but that he had decided that he could not accept the stated mission of the college." These discussions, a board officer reported, "led to a new sense of our mission and its influence on the college." Since then the college has hired several non-Christians who "were able to live with the stated mission."

Better boards evaluated curricular recommendations squarely within the context of the college's mission and considered either explicitly or indirectly whether proposals "made sense" and "fit" the college's central purposes. Less-effective boards tended to discuss various propositions outside the context of mission and *solely* from the perspective of a marketplace orientation fixed on the financial bottom line without regard for any deeper institutional vision.

These tendencies are graphically illustrated by the accounts of two trustees on very different boards, each confronted with proposals for curricular changes. In the first instance, the faculty of a historically church-related college voted to eliminate required Bible courses, an action that, predictably enough, troubled the board. The chairman of the board's development committee recounted:

> We were shocked by the faculty's announcement that they had decided to eliminate these requirements. Since it was founded by the denomination, courses in Bible have always been important for our students. We decided not to act hastily, to take some time to consider the issue. The president helped us to put the issue into the framework of the mission of the college. We decided to initiate a review of the college mission and purpose and to invite the faculty to join us in these efforts. The joint committee held several long meetings with trustees and faculty members and reworked the college's mission statement. . . . I think we're coming together on some compromises that will be acceptable to almost everyone.

With the president's assistance, the board was able to deliberate about a curriculum decision within the larger and critical context of the college's mission. "It's important," stated this board chairman, "that everyone be clear about our mission." In discussing the same incident in a separate interview, the president praised the trustees' handling of this situation. "The board was opposed to the elimination of Bible courses. To their credit, they challenged the faculty to show how the curriculum could meet the mission of the college, as set forth in the mission statement, without this component."

In the second case, a president recommended to the board that the college's astronomy program be discontinued due to excessive costs and low enrollments. One trustee explained:

> You have to understand that this event, dropping astronomy, is like M.I.T. dropping engineering. . . . No one on the board saw the market for the program. It was a financial decision. . . . Despite sentiment, despite the fact that the college's greatest president was an astronomer, and that we had an observatory, and a field station, the board stood its ground. Why is this an example of an effective decision? I don't really know. The board thought the facts were there, that this was the right thing to do.

The decision to terminate the astronomy program may ultimately have been justifiable; that is not the issue here. Of more immediate concern was the board's treatment of the question *solely* as a budgetary or economic matter. There was no sense that this decision, even if financially necessary, had any more profound implications for the college's mission, image, heritage, and hallmarks that had to be considered. More effective boards do not suffer such blind spots.

Likewise, less effective boards often agreed to pursue almost any program that had a glimmer of economic potential, again without regard to the match with the college's mission or the consequences for the institution's self-identity. A member of one such board confessed, "We're searching for and open to anything that will help us survive." A fellow trustee independently confirmed that, "We are trying to start up some new programs that will generate money."

How different this approach is from that of boards of other colleges in the study, which first considered the compatibility of any proposed new ventures with the institution's stated mission. Thus, the board of one college dedicated to world peace and brotherhood approved in concept the establishment of an international high school as a way to further the school's mission and not to corner some market. Another board decided that its president's vision for the future, which stressed only business programs and a new M.S. in management, was inadequate because it was "too marked a departure from our traditional liberal-arts values." In a similar vein, a trustee of yet another strong board reported that the college's efforts to develop programs in business, communications, and architecture led to "some tension with accrediting associations in these areas over our insistence on more liberal studies in each program in place of the things they want that seem more oriented to specific skills and techniques." All of these boards appreciated the need to match programs with mission and not merely with markets.

In a crowded, competitive field like higher education, the prospects are not bright for institutions and boards without a mission-driven sense of direction. Chaffee's penetrating 1984 study, "Successful Strategic Management in Small Private Colleges," demonstrated that these institutions are not well-served over the long term by strategies designed principally to cut costs, respond to the marketplace, and increase the flow of resources. However useful the efforts were to reduce inefficiencies, trim staff, add programs, teach off-campus, and open new markets, these tactics alone were insufficient. The more resilient colleges, while selectively opportunistic, emphasized an "interpretive" approach that invested heavily in "conceptual and communication systems" and the "management of meaning." Successful turnarounds occurred where the college's leadership clarified the institution's purposes and priorities and emphasized institutional credibility, integrity, and dignity. Where the adaptive and interpretive approaches conflicted, Chaffee concluded that "the interpretive strategy should take precedence" (p. 229). If so, trustees of precariously situated colleges should be much more attuned to the fundamental question posed by an interpretive strategy, "Why are we together?" than by the basic question of an adaptive strategy, "What are we doing?" Stated another way, boards of trustees must attend to the management of meaning and mission in order to ensure an institution's vitality.

On the matter of mission, then, trustees of colleges and universities might do well to follow Drucker's advice. In an article titled "What Business Can Learn from Nonprofits," Drucker (1989, p. 89) cited as the first lesson that the point of departure for all strategic plans should be performance of mission. Starting with the mission

> focuses the organization on action. It defines the specific strategies needed to attain crucial goals. It creates a disciplined organization. It alone can prevent the most common degenerative disease of organizations, especially large ones: splintering their always limited resources on things that are "interesting" or look "profitable" rather than concentrating them on a very small number of productive efforts. The best nonprofits devote a great deal of thought to defining their organization's mission.

3. The board's decisions and actions reflect and reinforce institutional values.

Lawrence Butler, a senior associate of the Cheswick Center, a Boston-based organization that specializes in board development, likened the board to "the nucleus of a cell in which is preserved the DNA of the organism. It passes the genetic code along to each successive generation. . . . To be assured that the underlying values in the organization's genetic code are preserved intact, the board has a special role to play" (personal communication, June 27, 1990). Boards hold a great deal in trust, such as the organization's reputation, financial assets, physical plant, and human resources. The most precious asset entrusted to the board, however, may be the institution's values and beliefs. As Carver (1990, p. 19) maintained, "The governing board is a guardian of organizational values. . . . Endless discussions about events cannot substitute for deliberations and explicit pronouncements on values." Nor, we would add, can "explicit pronouncements" substitute for board *actions* that epitomize the organization's values.

Institutional values shape the policies, strategies, and tactics—the means—to achieve the desired ends expressed in a college's statement of purpose. As was the case with mission statements, effective boards were both more enlightened about institutional values and more likely to apply that knowledge to the decisions at hand. In other words, the decisions of effective boards reflected and reinforced the college's espoused values, beliefs, and philosophy.

We asked trustees, "What are the core values or beliefs of this college? That is, what does this college stand for?" The question puzzled many members of weaker boards. "I can't think of any core values of the college," confessed the chairman of one board. "Maybe that's because I have no ties." Another trustee of the same institution noted only that the college "used to have a lot of catchwords or slogans." Trustees of midrange boards tended to offer brief yet informative responses such as "community service," "service to society," and "Christian morality." However, the most profound and most replete responses were offered by members of effective boards.

> The whole approach here is different. We are caring and concerned. We have a shared vision of what the college should be. Others don't have as much emphasis on values, spiritual values. . . . This college stands for things important to me: world peace, improved race relations, international understanding.

Added a fellow board member, "We have an important commitment to the campus community as a family." On another effective board, the values articulated by trustees concerned opportunities for students to reach maximum potential, to be self-directed learners and independent thinkers, and to promote the importance of the individual and responsibility to the community.

The contrast between effective and ineffective boards was even more sharply drawn when the line of inquiry about values shifted from words to deeds. Interviewees were asked to "describe a situation where a board decision or action was shaped by and in turn reflected a core value" of the college. Trustees unable to identify any core values in the first place were, of course, unable to provide any relevant illustrations either. Members of somewhat stronger boards cited decisions such as the opening of a new downtown facility to serve the business community, the establishment of an interdenominational center, and an increased emphasis on ethics in the business school curriculum as examples of decisions that enacted organizational values.

The richest and most eloquent testimony about the connections between institutional values and institutional decisions were offered by trustees of one of the most effective boards we visited. One case concerned divestment, the other concerned alcohol. The discussion about divestment, reported the board chairman, was always within the context of the purposes of the institution and not just a question of economics. It concerned the college's ties to the denomination's holdings and viewpoint. The discussion was nearly always with reference to the institution. . . . The board kept the issue related to the college's purpose.

The board treated the issue of drinking the same way. Although college regulations prohibited the consumption of alcohol on campus, the policy was occasionally breached. The board and the president were in a quandary. To ignore the use of alcohol was contrary to the college's creed and therefore unacceptable to many board members. At the same time, the board was reluctant to require that students report violations by fellow students for adjudication by the campus judicial committee for fear that such a policy would adversely affect relationships among students and erode a carefully cultivated sense of community. The college had no desire to transform students into informants. What to do? As reported by the president, two deeply religious trustees indicated at a board meeting that

> they had been impressed by the counseling approach to alcohol abuse, work-
> ing with students on alcohol problems, rather than prosecuting them. They
> saw this approach as consistent with an educational institution and consistent
> with rehabilitation and religious purpose. Here were two trustees who opened
> their minds, spent time on campus, interpreted a consensus point of view and
> persuaded the board. . . . The key was to take the onus off students who
> reported violators and could now be seen as helpers with an opportunity to be
> constructive, to help someone obtain counseling. . . . We wanted a community
> ethic consistent with supporting a religious society.

As regards both divestment and alcohol, the board constructed policies on the cornerstone of institutional values.

By comparison, a midrange board confronted the question of alcohol abuse "because we needed to do something about vandalism and potential liability problems," a very different and more utilitarian motive. As one trustee stated, "I think the policy is successful because students didn't complain about it at today's board meeting and because vandalism has been reduced." These policy objectives were far more instrumental and less normative than the aims and decisions articulated by members of the more effective board.

In addition to board decisions as a means to convey institutional values, the very *behavior* of effective boards clearly manifested the trustees' intentions to embody a corporate philosophy or creed. On effective boards, trustees individually and collectively tended to personify the "organizational saga" (Clark, 1970), the core values and concepts that furnish a source of direction and purpose for distinctive colleges. Frequently, these behaviors included highly symbolic acts: the regular inclusion of faculty at board retreats, the appointment of a woman to chair the board of a woman's college, a decision to forego reappointment to the board in order to enable "younger people to come onto the board," and the anonymous payment of tuition and expenses for several needy students a year.

Perhaps the most emblematic behaviors by boards were revealed by critical incidents with presidents, both at the time of appointment and at the moment of departure. One dramatic example occurred when the trustees of one college with an effective board were confronted with campus unrest over the selection of the search committee's second choice to be the new president. On many campuses the board might not even consent to meet with upset students and faculty to discuss the process. An alumna trustee explained, however, why the board agreed, at the suggestion of the acting president, to have an open meeting with students.

> The critical time was between the selection of the new president and his arrival. There was a lot of misunderstanding among faculty and students. . . . The action of the board created a perception of mistrust. The best thing we did was listen. We explained why the choice was a good one. We responded to questions. I have no recollection of discussing any candidate's drawbacks or making direct comparisons. . . . We talk about being a community. This was a case where the board could not be above or separate from the community. Being here, talking with students, was the board's way of taking its place in the community.

In short, the board practiced what it preached. The college was a community where the exchange of viewpoints, even on a matter as delicate as the selection of a new president, was welcome and vital to sustain harmony and to maintain trust. There was, incidentally, another important and astute reason for the board's action, as this same trustee explained. "It was in our hands to defuse the controversy as much as possible before the new president arrived. We created a conducive environment for the president to succeed. We handled some very important stage setting."

Trustee actions at the other end of a president's tenure also disclosed a great deal about a board's values. Several years ago the CEO of one college developed Alzheimer's disease but was not aware of his deterioration. As a relative newcomer to the board reported:

> A few of the senior trustees noticed his condition and quietly arranged for him to get some medical attention. They didn't embarrass him or create any disruption for the college. It was all handled very discreetly, quietly, and no one was upset. Stability was maintained for the college, and arrangements were made for his retirement and care. I wasn't a part of that process, but I came into an atmosphere of concern for others and for the college that those trustees had developed and sustained.

In acting responsibly, judiciously, and humanely, the board exemplified the college's commitment to personal dignity and a caring environment.

Elsewhere, a less effective board decided summarily to remove the president. There were only token efforts to resolve the matter privately and amicably and no consultation or communication with campus leaders before or after the president's dismissal. The announcement ensnared the board in an ugly, public campaign, complete with banners and buttons, to save the CEO. Whatever the merits of the case, the board's actions throughout hardly reinforced the stated values of this church-related college. Suddenly, the rhetoric about the college's commitment to human dignity and mutual respect seemed hollow. And what lessons about values were students and faculty to draw from a precipitous, unilateral, and ultimately abortive attempt by the chairman of an ineffective board to discharge the president? Stopped by the executive committee and asked to resign, the chairman refused and remained in office, though not on speaking terms with the president. Eventually, both resigned.

As these examples highlight, more effective boards appreciated the symbolic and moral dimensions of policy decisions and board behavior as occasions to affirm, communicate, and reflect institutional values. Decisions and actions were consciously intended to uphold a value system while solving a problem. Less effective boards were prone to overlook or even contravene the relationship between institutional values and board behavior. These trustees did not see any inherent contradictions when, for instance, a homogeneous board issued a call to arms for affirmative action or when a board nobly proclaimed the primacy of the academic mission and then appeared on campus only to attend athletic events. Actions such as these served both to undermine the board's credibility and to betray the college's espoused principles. However inadvertently, the unmistakable message from the board to the campus community was "Do as we say, not as we do."

SUGGESTIONS

Just over 95 percent of all college trustees have earned a college degree (AGB, 1985). However valuable, that experience alone does not equip people to serve as college trustees any more than flying frequently prepares someone to serve on the board of directors of an airline. As the accounts of effective board members attest, a trustee also needs to understand rather deeply the organization's culture and nature.

Curiously, though, the standard elements of orientation sessions for new trustees and board-development activities for experienced trustees tend to overlook or downplay discussions of organizational context. Orientation programs normally include a review of the board's bylaws, committees, roles, and responsibilities, an overview of major administrative areas, and a tour of the campus. Few orientations systematically address the distinctive characteristics of academic organizations or imbue trustees with an intimate sense of that college's particular heritage, history, values, and meaning. The data from this study suggest, however, that all trustees, even alumni or longtime acquaintances of the college and veterans of the board, would benefit periodically from such a program. What might be the principal aims of such an orientation?

To Describe the Academic Culture. Obviously enough, full-time professors are probably most qualified to convey a sense of the academic culture. Thus, the president might invite a faculty leader, perhaps a past or present chair of the campus senate, to explain to new trustees the concept of shared governance and the scope and operations of the campus senate. A student leader could provide a similar overview of student government. A senior professor or department chair might describe how the consultation process functions to reach consensus on academic matters. In fact, a relatively recent policy decision, at the campus or departmental level, might be presented as a case study to illuminate the decision-making process. Another professor might discuss academic freedom and sketch the work life of a faculty member: how research unfolds, how courses and curricula are developed, how peers are evaluated, what yields satisfaction, and what produces frustration. Lay trustees are no more apt to have much prior knowledge about these phenomena than an academic appointed to a corporate board could be expected to already understand a company's design, manufacturing, and decision-making processes.

One way to ensure that seasoned trustees are *re*socialized to the academic culture is to involve them in the orientation of new board members. Moreover, as one trustee observed, the participation of veteran trustees in the orientation program "sets an example," transmits a "fierce loyalty to the university," and demonstrates the board's willingness to "dedicate time" to the institution. An experienced trustee, therefore, might be asked to highlight the most distinctive features of the academic landscape from a board member's viewpoint. In addition, newcomers might be furnished a brief description of the chief differences between colleges and corporations. (See, for example, Baldridge et al., 1978, chapter 2; Chait, 1979. For trustees of research universities, Cohen and March, 1974, chapter 3 might be especially useful.) As we noted previously, many trustees do not fully grasp the prevalent norms of academe until after several years' service on the board. Why not adopt measures that shorten this time line and thus enable a trustee to be constructive more quickly?

To Impart a Sense of Institutional History. To better understand the contemporary context, trustees should have some appreciation for the organization's past. As Robert Lynn, then senior vice president of the Lilly Endowment, cautioned, "An institution whose leaders are out of touch with its movement through time—its trajectory—is often in serious difficulty. Historical amnesia is always debilitating and occasionally fatal" (Lilly,

1989, section 1, p. 2). Nevertheless, most board members are largely unfamiliar with their institution's history. In fact, a good many could not even remember the college's priorities three years ago.

There are several ways to remedy this deficiency. First, if a college history exists, it should be the first item each new trustee receives. The college's resident historian (and there always seems to be one) could discuss one or two crucial themes at an orientation session. To further enliven the process and, again, to resocialize others, the board or the president might prevail upon a few senior or retired trustees or professors to recount firsthand some of the institution's monumental moments and decisions. These remarks might be videotaped both to preserve the college's oral history and to present to future members of the board. A sense of chronology can also be communicated visually through an institutional time line that depicts key events in the college's history.

To Convey Institutional Values. Along with a sense of the organization's history, trustees need a sense of the college's ethos, or "soul," those values and principles that undergird, drive, and give meaning to the institution's mission. A wise trustee of an exemplary board advised, "It is important that board members know the institution, know the facts, do their homework, and have a feel for the college's spirit in order to share the vision of the campus community."

Toward that end, newcomers might be provided with a list of the college's dominant values and hallmark characteristics as compiled from a formal or informal survey of the institution's key constituencies. While such lists are useful, stories and anecdotes are even more powerful. Nearly every college has some vignettes and lore that capture the essence of the organization. These stories should be captured in a booklet distributed to *all* newcomers to the board, faculty, and staff, and recounted directly to new trustees, if at all possible by some of the people who actually experienced them. Likewise, most campuses are blessed with at least a few individuals who are a "walking embodiment" of the very heart and soul of the institution. New and old trustees (and new presidents) should be afforded regular occasions to listen to these legendary members speak about the college's bedrock values and glorious moments.

As a result of these activities, new trustees should be well-versed about the academic culture as a whole and also about an institution's peculiar history and distinctive characteristics. New trustees would thus enter what Bellah et al. (1985, p. 153) termed a "community of memory, one that does not forget its past."

> In order not to forget that past, a community is involved in retelling its story, its constitutive narrative, and in so doing, it offers examples of the men and women who have embodied and exemplified the meaning of the community.

These stories of collective history and exemplary individuals are an important part of the tradition that is so central to a community of memory.

To sustain that sense of shared history, each board meeting might start by reading a statement on institutional values or the board's role, or by retelling an instructive anecdote from the college's history. This idea may strike some trustees as too contrived or ceremonial. These skeptics might ponder, however, why most sports events start with the national anthem, why school children are required to recite the Pledge of Allegiance daily, or why the liturgies of most religious groups always include (and often repeat within the same service) certain basic prayers. The answer, of course, is to socialize and *re*socialize people to a shared set of living values.

With a heightened and ingrained awareness of the college's culture and context, trustees can more readily evaluate recommendations and imminent actions as *statements of values*. In other words, effective boards consciously and expressly consider the symbolic content and moral message inherent in any proposed course of action. "What," the board will ask instinctively and explicitly, "will this decision communicate about our college's principles and priorities? Will the board's action reflect and reinforce our institution's espoused values, or will we appear to be inconsistent or even hypocritical?" Boards should routinely raise and answer these questions prior to any major policy decisions. If not, others surely will, and frequently under far more difficult circumstances for the board and the president.

DISCUSSION QUESTIONS AND EXERCISES

1. Ask each board member to list three traits that best describe the organization's culture or personality and three values that are at the core of the college's belief system. Collate the lists and discuss. Seek ways individually or collectively to discuss or exchange responses with trustees of other colleges or nonprofit organizations in order to determine whether your lists are truly distinctive.

2. Guided by the administration, review the range of the college's activities, programs, and audiences and then *infer* the actual emphases of the institution's mission. How well does the inferential mission match the expressed mission? A related activity, developed by the Lilly Endowment Leadership Education Program, would be to ask the board to provide answers to three questions: What do we believe? Whom do we serve? What do we do? The responses could be listed and compared for consistency.

3. Describe a key action or decision by the board that reflected and reinforced a core organizational value. In taking this action or reaching this decision, did the board explicitly discuss the matter of values beforehand, was it implicit in the discussion, or was it only afterward that you realized how much the decision was influenced by a deeply held value? What steps can the board take to ensure that values and history are explicitly considered before actions are taken?

4. Meet every year or two, as arranged by the president and senior staff, with faculty and students to discuss why they chose to become (or remain) a part of your "community of memory." Find out what the college *means* to them.

2

The Educational Dimension

DEFINITION

Competency 2 concerns the **educational dimension** of trusteeship. Effective boards take the necessary steps to ensure that trustees are well-informed about the institution and about the board's roles, responsibilities, and performance. As self-directed learners, strong boards: (1) consciously create opportunities for trustee education; (2) regularly seek feedback on the board's performance; and (3) pause periodically for self-reflection, especially to examine the board's mistakes.

DESCRIPTIONS

The Board Creates Numerous Opportunities for Trustee Education. In a study of work groups, Hackman and Walton (1986, p. 83) concluded that a supportive organizational context included an educational system that provided members with the necessary technical assistance and knowledge to perform capably. As a type of work group, boards of trustees also require a shared knowledge base to function effectively. In other words, boards have a lot to learn. Ironically, many colleges do very little to teach trustees, even though the institutions themselves exist to educate. Just as the shoemaker's shoes are the last ones soled, in too many instances, and especially on campuses with ineffective boards, trustees are apparently the last ones taught.

Less effective boards tended to assume that prior (though not always relevant) experience as a college student, as a board member elsewhere, or as an executive had equipped trustees with nearly all the knowledge needed to be a competent board member. The operative assumption seemed to be that successful corporate, professional, or religious leaders, almost by definition, did not need to be oriented to the college or to the board's roles and responsibilities. Weaker boards further supposed that any minor deficits in the preparation of some of their trustees would be quickly filled by on-the-job experience. "There's no formal preparation," commented a trustee on a comparatively weak board. "It's all informal. Basically, the president seeks out people who are already prepared for this role." A trustee on a particularly ineffective board asked incredulously, "Is there any such thing as formal preparation for this role? We certainly could use it, if there is. I don't know of anything. No guidelines or anything like that were ever given to me." Numerous trustees cited "osmosis" as the principal form of education. A common experience, as reported by one trustee of a midrange board, was that "the college tosses a few pieces of literature at you and assumes you'll pick up the rest. I'd give them a C or C minus in trustee training."

To dramatize the inadequacy of this approach, trustees (and college presidents) might consider the situation in reverse. Imagine that a college president had been appointed to the board of directors of a tire-and-rubber company. The CEO of the company mailed the president copies of the company's latest annual report, financial audit, and a statement of director responsibilities. In addition, one of the CEO's deputies arranged for the president a daylong site visit to corporate headquarters that included a tour one of the company's nearby plants, a series of half-hour meetings with senior managers, and an introduction to the union's leaders. Is this college president, who has kicked some tires along the way, now well-prepared to serve on the company's board (Chait, 1990, p. 26)? The same question might be asked about a corporate executive provided an equally cursory orientation to a college.

More effective college boards did not leave trustee orientation to chance or passively rely on the distribution of information packets. In their efforts to acclimate trustees to a distinct role in a particular environment, both presidents and trustees regarded the CEO's role as orienter and educator to be essential. Thus, one president mused, "As a group the board is learning how to provide governance and leadership. I have an enormous teaching role to fill with the board. It is curious to be in the role of teacher to one's employer, isn't it?" However unusual the role reversal may be, trustees on effective boards appreciated the president's readiness to play the teacher's part. As a longtime member of a stalwart board reminisced about his early days on the board:

> The past president was very helpful to me as a new trustee. He'd stay after board meetings and talk with me extensively about what had been discussed in

the meetings, why positions were being taken, how the group process had
worked, how I could find ways to participate more effectively.

For members of an equally superb board, which had a daylong introduction
to the college's mission and programs, the most valuable component of
trustee education was also the opportunity to learn from the president. "He
spends a lot of time individually with each new member explaining the
expectations of the role of trustee."

Among the other practices cited by trustees as helpful for neophytes were
individual conversations with the board chair, a "tutorial" with the trea-
surer, classroom visits, and educational and social functions with faculty
leaders. One exemplary board furnished new trustees with "some booklets
and AGB training materials to read at home" *and* "followed up in a seminar
with some discussions of the main points as they are applied here." Two
midrange boards depended on experienced trustees to mentor newcomers.
"We appoint someone," explained the chair-elect of one of these boards,
"who has served for a while to be a guide to the newcomer and to be
available to answer questions."

For stronger boards, this educational process did not end with orientation. Rather, the board's efforts to learn and to improve were continuous.
Indeed, to return to a central theme of chapter 1, the board's visible
commitment to learn personified and buttressed a central institutional
goal: education.

Members of proficient boards frequently mentioned various instances of
trustee education, beyond orientation sessions, that enabled the board to
perform more effectively. Often at the president's suggestion, many trustees
attended national conferences or workshops aimed at trustees, or perused
relevant periodicals such as *AGB Reports* and *The Chronicle of Higher
Education*. In an extraordinary example of an institutional commitment to
trustee education, an exceptional board charged the members of its development committee to become well-versed on the issue of divestment in order to
lead an enlightened discussion of the topic among members of the campus
community. Several of these trustees traveled to New York to meet with
officers of corporations with operations in South Africa and with representatives of advocacy organizations on both sides of the question. "Because the
board members genuinely educated themselves about divestment," the president observed, "they moved into a position of leadership" on the issue.

Effective and midrange boards often designed and conducted their own
seminars on topics of special interest to them. The subject matter spanned
from mission, goals, and long-range plans to finances, the budget process,
and endowment management. Although most boards scheduled these sessions sporadically, one has a two-day retreat every summer to probe one or
two major educational issues—such as the goals of general education or the
future of graduate education—in some depth. A midrange board recently
decided to have a "training component" at every board meeting. "At one

meeting," the president reported, "we talked about the role of the board. Another time I explained what enrollment management is and how we can apply it to our situation."

All of these different formats and topics served a common objective: to better educate the board on matters vital to the college's future. The payoffs from trustee seminars were substantial, as evidenced by the enthusiastic assessment offered by the chairman of an effective board:

> I'm really proud of how far the board has come in its understanding of financial issues. Three or four years ago a number of board members felt that we weren't getting the kind of detailed financial data we needed. We simply didn't understand the college's financial situation well enough to be confident that it was in good shape. . . . The then board chair, fiscal affairs committee, and the president decided to hold a board retreat to teach the board about fiscal affairs. We learned about budgeting, financial ratios, and other techniques. Not only did we learn a lot, but the retreat also raised the president's sight about financial issues and means of communicating more effectively with the board. I think the retreat was our first step toward becoming better informed and more skillful financial stewards of the college. . . . I think we were effective because we tried to learn more about an important board responsibility. Anytime we can do that we've taken a step in the right direction.

The Board Periodically Engages in Self-Reflection and Seeks Feedback on Its Performance. The educational activities of competent boards were not limited to substantive institutional matters, as important as those issues were. Better boards also devised means to learn more about the board's *process*—the way the board did its business. In a particularly perceptive article on corporate boards, Alderfer (1986, p. 50) asserted that a "key factor" of effective boards was the presence of "an active mechanism for the board to review its own structure and process." The most capable corporate boards in that study were more aware of their own behavior and more cognizant of their performance as a unit. Consequently, those boards were better equipped to detect their deficiencies and appropriately refine their operations.

Boards of trustees of colleges (and other not-for-profits, for that matter) have no less a need to be introspective. And, in fact, effective boards, far more often than weaker boards, utilized retreats and other means to stimulate self-examination. Comments by two trustees of competent boards illustrate the dividends these sessions yielded:

> We had a retreat recently with some people from the Association of Governing Boards to help us with a self-study process. That was a candid reflection on our needs and concerns as a board. It led to some changes in our committee structure and to a recognition of our need to bring in some new skills and diversity to our board.

We have had wonderful retreats, something inspirational as well as academic. We had a talk on spiritual values, about why we want to be what we are. There are lots of self-studies here. We are really coming to grip with values.

In yet another case, the incumbent chairperson asked the chair-designate how he would like to prepare for the position. Convinced that the board's processes, paper flow, and committee performance could be improved, the incoming chair recommended a self-evaluation followed by a retreat. "What grew out of the self-study," the president related, "was a set of major changes in the way the board does business." Among the most noteworthy modifications was that "board officers were charged with making presentations rather than just listening to administrators make them."

In contrast to these productive and reflective events, the then chairman of a markedly ineffective board attempted to organize a retreat to "assess our failures and successes," but there was so little support for the idea that "I couldn't get it going." The matter was dropped, and more than three years have passed without even a superficial attempt at self-assessment by the board.

Retreats are by design occasional, and sometimes landmark, events. Thus, effective boards employed other methods to be introspective on a more routine basis, and the board chair often played an instrumental role in the process. A critical function of a group leader, according to one study (Hackman and Walton, pp. 89, 103), is to monitor the team's performance, in part by asking one's self diagnostic questions such as: Does the team have a supportive organizational context? Are ample coaching and process assistance available? Are there signs of problems in the task work or in the members' ability to work together? Sensitive to this responsibility, the former chairman of a strong board explained,

> I guess I have some personal standards I use to monitor our performance, such as, "Is the board addressing the crucial issues? Is it taking the time to examine them thoroughly? Does it then come to a thoughtful and constructive conclusion on the issues?"

The chairman of another able board decided to monitor the group's performance in part by asking the trustees to complete a brief questionnaire. The responses disclosed that a few trustees "felt that they didn't have extensive opportunities to influence our decisions." Consequently, the chairman modified his own behavior.

> You can't force people to talk, but I remind myself that it is crucial to make sure that there are ample opportunities, to watch for the person who may be sitting there quietly, not to assume that his concerns have been represented around the table. So I'm trying to draw each individual out and make sure that his views are heard.

When the board's leadership, especially the chair and the president, poses and encourages reflective questions, that behavior invites other trustees to also raise questions about the board's performance and individual trustee roles. There are, as a result, fewer "nondiscussable" topics and "improper" questions about the board's operations.

In less introspective boardrooms, trustees were more disposed to swallow criticisms and concerns and thus allow a silent yet widespread exasperation to fester. A dysfunctional politeness eventually takes hold wherein most board members plainly recognize a serious problem with the board's functioning, but few if any feel comfortable enough to broach the issue. Everyone on the board leaves the meeting puzzled as to why no one stated the obvious. As one member of a weak board lamented, "There's no evaluation or feedback at all. No one knows if he's doing what needs to be done or not. As a result, we are floundering and have no clout. . . . If I ran my business like that, we'd be bankrupt or I'd be gone quickly. It's embarrassing." The same syndrome can afflict outside directors on corporate boards, according to a study conducted at the Harvard Business School. Lorsch (1989, p. 182) determined that:

> As long as directors avoid discussing fundamental premises and goals, as long as they restrict criticism to pointed questions, and as long as they are unwilling to converse freely, in or out of meetings, with fellow directors, they will continue to dissipate the power of their numerical superiority. Open dialogue with one another and with the CEO is crucial for an ability to govern and, as we've documented, will allow directors to identify potential problems more quickly.

Despite the advantages of introspection and evaluation, remarkably few boards have any regular processes to gather and discuss performance feedback on the board as a whole or on individual trustees. The absence of such data can significantly hinder effectiveness. Studies of workers (Lawler, 1973), groups (Zander, 1982), and boards (Houle, 1989) all found that periodic appraisals were a constructive means to motivate and enhance performance. Exercising "the capacity for self-criticism," Houle concluded, "is the surest impetus for improving the quality of the board and the work it does" (p. 157). Without such information, trustees will have a limited sense of the board's impact, and the group will have no more incentive to improve than a team engaged in a game where no one kept score or followed the rules. Zander (p. 113) explained:

> When members get no feedback on their group's performance, therefore, they tend to believe that the output of their group has been good, that they can be satisfied the unit has succeeded. Members who get little feedback also expect their group will do well in days to come and do not fear failure. No news is good news.

Why did so many incapable boards eschew performance feedback? Three arguments against trustee evaluations were advanced by members of less effective boards.

1. Lack of time. "There has been a series of crises in recent years, making it difficult for the group to function. . . . We haven't had time to evaluate the board."

2. Lack of compensation. "I haven't told anyone they're doing a rotten job. All of this is voluntary, no one is getting paid for it. We appreciate any shared interest. It's not like other boards where you are getting paid."

3. Lack of results. "Self-evaluation is almost useless. . . . There will be too many compromises. Everybody has a little ax to grind; it would be valueless."

Evidently less swayed by such arguments, some midrange and effective boards periodically monitored their group's performance. At a basic level, the evaluations concerned trustee attendance, preparedness, and involvement and, as a rule, the chairperson communicated informally with the laggards. An exceptional board broadened the concept to include an informal assessment of "the quality of the decisions we are making" and whether we "walk out of meetings with questions about what we did." A few other boards used more extensive processes, usually managed by the nominating committee. In one case, for instance, that committee annually conducted "an informal evaluation of the performance of each trustee and used that information in recommending appointments and assignments." Two other skillful boards extended the process in order to receive feedback "from those looking for leadership," as one chairman referred to the trustees' key constituencies on campus. Hence, these boards intermittently and casually consulted with senior faculty and senior administrators, especially with respect to the effectiveness of board committees. While the feedback was intrinsically useful to the board, the process also supported the norms of consultation and added to a favorable political climate. And, as a very practical matter, boards that have some sort of evaluation process can more legitimately ask that faculty and staff be attentive to assessment, too—an important consideration if the press for faculty and staff accountability continues to intensify.

The Board Learns from Its Mistakes. A recent study (McCall et al., 1988, p. 88) revealed that "business mistakes, in which bad judgment and poor decisions led to failure" provided important "learning thrusts" that were an integral part of "how successful executives develop on the job." The authors reported that "most of the executives we interviewed confessed to having made at least one (and sometimes several) serious business mistakes in their careers (p. 106)." The best ones learned a crucial lesson as a result.

Effective boards of trustees also made mistakes and, like successful executives, they were able to extract from their errors and hardships important lessons about how to improve their performance. Their less capable counterparts treated setbacks as little more than embarrassing lapses, best forgotten.

When asked to describe the greatest mistake the board had made in the past two or three years, there was a clear pattern of difference among the trustees' responses. The least effective boards were the least likely to identify a substantial mistake. "We've made no big mistakes," asserted the chairman of one such board. "None monumental in impact. On committees you average your losses; this allows the board to move along without major errors." (This observation has special significance because the chairman had attempted unilaterally and unsuccessfully to oust the president.) Two members of an equally ineffective board stated: "I don't know of any large mistake." "Maybe, not pushing fund-raising. Is the board aware of that? Probably not." And, finally, even the president of one college with an incapable board purported, "Honestly and truthfully, I can't think of any mistake my board has made."

Middle-range boards could cite some mistakes, though often of a relatively minor nature, such as awarding an honorary degree to a controversial figure or signing an unduly restrictive contract with another organization. Sometimes spontaneously, other times prompted by the interviewer, trustees on midrange boards were able to articulate a general conclusion or lesson that they had learned from their mistake. In the two examples cited above the lessons gleaned were, respectively, "what free speech means" and to be "more attentive to the fine print."

The responses by members of effective boards were very different. These trustees freely described a significant mistake and consistently *volunteered* a rather lengthy and rich explanation of the lessons and implications derived from a particular setback. Consider, for example, the story of a board whose confidence in the president started to erode after a difficult and sometimes contentious first year. "It was a very painful time for us," recalled the chairman of the development committee. "We didn't know what to do." At the suggestion of a veteran trustee and former college president, the board engaged a consultant to conduct an evaluation of the president. However,

> when the report came out, it was clear that the major problems were with the board, not the president. We had been so fragmented that we couldn't provide a clear framework within which the president could manage. We simply had to stop seeing ourselves as independent individuals and come to understand what it means to be a group. . . . Our worst mistake was not having given the president a solid foundation right from the start. We didn't know how to give the president the orientation, the protection, and the support that was needed. . . . It was difficult but we have grown tremendously because of that

process. Now the board is much more cohesive and unified. . . . It seems clear that we are finally learning what it means to be a unified board that can govern the college effectively.

Thus, a once rather average board learned some significant new behaviors by reflecting upon some distressing mistakes it had made. By the time we visited the college a couple of years later, this board's performance had improved sufficiently to be unquestionably categorized as effective.

Another incident, with a very different focus, had an equally instructive outcome for the board. This college accepted a government grant to initiate a nursing program. Although the need for nurses had been well documented by the college's staff, the market study failed to examine why the field was less and less attractive to students, especially women. Enrollments were so woefully inadequate that the college decided to discontinue the program only a few years after it had been launched. While not a happy academic tale, "mistakes aren't so bad, if you learn something from them," noted the immediate past chairman of the board.

> That experience taught us how to study opportunities more critically, to examine all aspects of an issue more thoughtfully, to consider a range of environmental dimensions and influences before we get into something. It taught us to stick with what we can do well and not try to meet every need or respond to every opportunity that comes along.

We find particularly noteworthy that this lesson was echoed, without any prompting, by nearly every other trustee we interviewed on this board, as illustrated by these excerpts.

> We learned that we had to emphasize quality in a few things rather than quantity in many.

> We learned to control our growth and build on solid foundations, rather than trying to be all things to all people.

Fletcher Byrom, former CEO of Koppers, Inc., advised executives to "make sure you generate a reasonable number of mistakes" (Peters and Waterman, 1982, p. 14). As a variant on that theme, when a board of trustees commits a significant error, its members should ask "What have we learned from this mistake, and what should we do differently as a result?" This process requires a commitment to reflect candidly on the board's assumptions and behaviors and to make whatever changes may be necessary to ensure that the board does not commit the same mistake again. In this sense, the board must personify Schon's (1983) notion of the "reflective practitioner," someone able to reflect and act at the same time so that introspection informs action and vice versa. As the chairman of an effective board concluded, "Improving our board's effectiveness will involve . . . finding some ways to learn from our mistakes, to learn about our efforts and to improve them purposively."

SUGGESTIONS

In chapter 1 we outlined a curriculum for a trustee orientation heavily weighted toward issues of organizational norms and culture, and in chapter 7 we sketch a plan for a board retreat. Hence, the emphasis here will be on measures (in addition to those described earlier in this chapter) that a board can undertake routinely and as a complement to more extensive yet more occasional orientation programs and retreats. The educational activities we recommend provide a way to enlarge the board's scope of experience, and the feedback mechanisms offer a way to deepen the board's self-knowledge.

Conference Reports. Normally only a few members of any one board can attend the same national conferences or regional workshops, however useful these events may be. The costs in time and money are often too great. At best, therefore, a handful of trustees return with some new ideas and perspectives. In order to disseminate that information when trustees return from a seminar or workshop, the board could set aside a few minutes at its next full meeting for those individuals to summarize the program's highlights and to describe the "single best idea" they each heard. This practice will reinforce the notion that trustees are eager and able to learn from one another as well as from faculty and staff. In addition, knowing in advance that they will be asked to report to the board may encourage those who do attend conferences to listen just a little more closely and to ruminate just a little longer than they might otherwise have done.

Local Trustee Seminars. Rather than send a few of its trustees to a conference, a college could organize a local seminar for the entire board. This approach enables the board or an *ad hoc* agenda committee to select the most relevant topics, the most appropriate speakers, and the most convenient dates. Additionally, a local program permits the board to learn together, an important by-product that promotes group cohesion.

A tradition could be established that the board sets aside one day or two half-days a year for an in-depth discussion of a substantive educational issue based upon some common readings, with faculty and staff included as appropriate. Some sessions could focus on topics that increase the board's knowledge of the profession, such as academic tenure, affirmative action, student development, or student assessment. Others could deal with important trends, for example, on student demography, faculty supply and demand, or college costs. And still others could address the larger environment through a discussion of topics like the implications of a global economy or a technological revolution. In these latter sessions, some board members could certainly function more as expert resources than as lay trustees. On occasion, too, boards of nearby and comparable institutions might convene to consider together common concerns such as federal policy on student financial aid, state support for independent colleges, or the discontinuation of mandatory retirement. Over meals or between sessions, participants would have the opportunity to "talk shop" about trusteeship, an added benefit since most board members actually have a very limited sphere of knowledge about the governance of academic institutions.

Role-Related Discussion Groups. Just as the trustees of several neighboring institutions might profitably meet together now and then, so too might their board chairs. Presidents of comparable colleges meet all the time. Why shouldn't board chairs do the same? By virtue of their common role, board chairs have many similar concerns, such as how to support and advise the president, how to guide and lead discussions, how to energize committees, and how to orchestrate the work of trustee committees. The board chairs of the "seven sisters," the prestigious women's colleges of the northeast, meet periodically for such purposes. The concept could easily be broadened to include an informal meeting, say once a year, where the chairs of various board committees would confer with their counterparts from other nearby institutions to explore and learn more about how to fulfill a specific role more capably.

Rotating Committee Assignments. Lifelong job rotation is a trademark of the Japanese approach to management. This practice ensures that "virtually every department will have in it someone who knows the people, the problems, and the procedures of any other area within the organization. When coordination is necessary, both sides will be able to understand and cooperate with the other" (Ouchi, 1981, p. 32). Trustee committee rotation offers similar advantages to a board. Too often pigeon-holed as financial, investment, or academic specialists, many trustees serve on only one committee throughout their tenure and never learn to appreciate fully the interrelated concerns and constraints of other committees. New assignments will enhance trustee education, provide new challenges that may revitalize some board members, and eliminate the unfortunate stigma sometimes attached to a few committees of "secondary" importance, like student life or academic affairs, which typically do not attract as many corporate executives as the finance, investment, or physical plant committees do. Furthermore, experience on several different committees offers useful preparation for service in leadership roles on the board.

Internal Feedback Mechanisms. Fortunately, there are numerous techniques available to gather and communicate trustee perceptions of the board's performance. All of these methods are intended to help the board become more reflective and self-aware. Boards unfamiliar or ill at ease with introspection can start with the less intrusive measures and then augment the process as the trustees' needs and comfort level allow.

At the end of each board meeting, the chair might ask each trustee to write down (perhaps anonymously at first) on a five-by-seven index card any comments about the conduct of that meeting. Alternatively, the chair may ask some specific questions, such as: Did we spend our time on significant issues? Was the discussion constructive? Was there ample opportunity for everyone to contribute? Is there anything we can do to make our meetings more effective, more efficient, or more interesting? Do you feel we are deliberately avoiding some controversial but significant questions? The chair would collect the cards, analyze the responses with the president, and then report at a future meeting the findings and tenor of the group's comments and any modifications they would like to propose for consideration by the board. Using such an approach, individual trustees would be able to voice their concerns easily and early, before frustrations mounted. At the same time, the chair and president would profit from steady feedback on their efforts, and the board would be able to consider and adopt measures that improve its performance and forestall the development of larger problems.

As trustees habituate to this process, smaller boards especially may wish to dispense with the index cards and reserve about fifteen minutes or so at the end of a meeting for members to comment orally. Over time this procedure should become second nature to the board and an integral part of "the way we do things around here."

Beyond these measures to capture some "fast feedback" at each board meeting, boards might use a number of other mechanisms on a less frequent basis. If, as we recommend in the next chapter, a board of trustees sets annual goals for itself, then approximately once a year the trustees and the college's senior staff could review the board's progress toward the achievement of those ambitions. This approach would be, in effect, a "governance by objectives" version of the "management by objectives" technique widely used in the corporate sector.

A somewhat more analytical tool, the "critical incident technique" (Flanagan, 1954) has been fruitfully applied to performance appraisal for many years (Levinson, 1976; Boyatzis, 1982). The process rests upon a written, behavioral record of a critical incident produced by the actual participants, usually while detailed recollections of the event are still fresh in their minds. As applied to trusteeship, board members would be encouraged to write down now and then a rather precise description of how the board handled a particular situation, and whether they believed that behavior to be exemplary or inadequate. The reviews would be placed in an open file and then, perhaps with the assistance of an external facilitator, a few especially illuminating cases could be critically analyzed at a board seminar or retreat. The board would ask, "What can we learn from this incident and how can we put that learning to further use?" Critical incidents provide the advantages of richly contoured accounts of specific illustrations, a historical record to measure the board's progress, and a focus on behaviors (*how* the board acted) and not just on official actions (*what* the board decided).

Some boards enlarge the scope of responsibility of the nominating committee to include monitoring the board's performance and overall health. Such committees, sometimes renamed the committee on trusteeship, evaluate the effectiveness of other committees and the board's overall performance. This arrangement properly places the primary burden for assessing and improving the board where it belongs: with the board itself and not solely or even mainly on the shoulders of the president.

Members of the committee on trusteeship normally have confidential conversations with committee chairs to appraise the performance of committee members and vice versa. As necessary, a member of the committee meets informally with subpar performers to provide feedback and to offer some constructive suggestions. And, as detailed in the next chapter, the committee also helps identify those board members who are ready to assume positions of greater responsibility on the board.

Finally, boards might undertake a comprehensive self-study every couple of years as a way to obtain internal feedback. Such self-assessments often produce valuable information about the trustees' self-perceptions that can serve as a springboard for introspective discussions at a board retreat. Collated responses to the AGB *Self-Study Criteria* or the Cheswick Center Self-Rating Schedule (Savage, 1982), for example, can pinpoint those areas of responsibility and internal board operations where a majority of the trustees believe the board's performance could be substantially improved. A briefer questionnaire, developed as part of the present study, enables trustees to gauge and reflect upon the board's effectiveness on each of the six competencies we have identified as key dimensions of successful trusteeship.[1]

While helpful as a point of departure for reflective discussions, board members and presidents should realize that self-evaluations have limitations and potential blind spots. Trustees' self-perceptions and an objective, accurate appraisal of the board's performance are not one and the same. We analyzed data from sixty-one boards that completed the AGB self-study instrument (Chait and Taylor, 1987). There were extremely small variations among the scores, both from one board to another and across the responses of individual boards to the eleven criteria covered in the questionnaire. The self-evaluations seemed to suggest that most boards handled most responsibilities quite well. Yet, ample evidence exists that board performance varies vary widely among institutions (Taylor, 1987).

---

[1] Available from the Center for Higher Education Governance and Leadership, University of Maryland, College Park.

Why do trustee self-evaluations not differentiate performance levels more effectively?[2] Ashford (1989) concluded that self-assessments of any kind are almost universally inaccurate for several reasons. Briefly, these are:

- The environment provides limited and inconsistent performance standards. (Just what *is* effective trusteeship? Can anyone agree on appropriate standards, criteria, and evidence?)

- Feedback cues are difficult to interpret. (Signals, messages, and comments are often ambiguous and unclear, leaving trustees to wonder, "Now what's *that* supposed to mean?")

- Assessment data are frequently interpreted in a way to preserve one's ego and self-esteem. (Who could do better under these circumstances? What could the faculty [or some other critic] possibly know about effective trusteeship?)

To compound the problem still further, most trustees have not served on boards of drastically different competence. With a limited frame of reference and a narrow basis for comparison, most trustees' self-assessments are not likely to vary widely. For all these reasons, then, a board of trustees may wish to obtain some feedback from sources beyond its own membership. A few possible techniques follow, again starting with the least intrusive intervention.

External Feedback Mechanisms. From time to time the board might collect evaluative observations and suggestions from the president and from other senior staff members as well. Working closely with trustees and board committees, these administrators are especially well-situated to comment on the board's efficiency and effectiveness. Does the board (or a particular committee) grasp the major issues at hand? Does it focus on policy and strategy? Does it request a great deal of irrelevant information? Does it provide the necessary support and direction for senior management?

In light of the difficulties inherent in asking senior staff to evaluate their "employers," the board might invite an outside intermediary to interview the senior staff every year or two and then provide an anonymous composite of their remarks. However, even if a board follows this procedure, the chair, the executive committee, or the committee on trusteeship should discuss the board's performance face-to-face with the president at least annually.

The process of soliciting external feedback on the board's performance could be extended to include other constituencies, such as the faculty, students, and alumni. Since these groups tend to have far less interaction with

---

[2] Self-evaluations were similarly inaccurate when related to compensation decisions (Meyer, 1975).

the board, any surveys or interviews should focus less on an evaluation of the board's performance and more on recommendations to improve the board's communications and relationships with these audiences. In addition, the process could be designed to elicit from respondents would-be priorities for the board and areas that warrant greater attention on the part of trustees. The very fact that the board asks for such suggestions should have positive effects.

In a few cases corporate and nonprofit boards have retained outside experts to attend their meetings and to offer feedback on the way they do business. The observer, perhaps a seasoned trustee or a professional consultant, should concentrate chiefly on issues of group dynamics—participation, communication, and information flow—rather than on the substantive aspects of the board's agenda.

When he was mayor of New York City, Edward Koch habitually strolled the city's sidewalks asking constituents, "How am I doing?" Boards of trustees need not and should not go to such an extreme. The role of mayor and trustee are, after all, quite different. On the other hand, too few boards systematically ask themselves "How are we doing?" In the worst cases, the board does not even recognize the need for self-examination or the board construes the absence of crisis to be confirmation of its effectiveness.

In sum, the most reflective boards were also the most effective boards. Self-awareness, informed by periodic feedback from internal and external sources, enabled better boards to learn, to improve, and ultimately to celebrate their successes. And the achievement and recognition of group goals is an essential ingredient in building group cohesion, the third competency of effective boards.

DISCUSSION QUESTIONS AND EXERCISES

1. What are the key components of trustee education for your board? Are they intended primarily for newcomers on the board or are there also ongoing efforts directed at the board as a whole?

2. How does your board know how well it is doing? What criteria and standards does it apply? What sources of evidence does it use?

3. How does a member of your board *give* feedback on the board's performance? How does a board member *get* feedback?

4. What would you cite as the board's biggest mistake in the last three years or so? What did the board learn from this episode? Does it do anything differently as a result?

5. At a board retreat or special session, ask the senior staff and the trustees to meet separately. Each group would be asked to respond to the same question: What can the people in the other room do to help those of us

in this room fulfill our responsibilities more effectively? The groups would then reconvene and present, without specific attribution, their recommendations for consideration. This assignment provides a relatively safe way for each group to give feedback to the other.

6. The board of an independent secondary school several years ago instituted a playful yet useful idea to foster trustee education. Once or twice a year, the board chair administers a "pop quiz," a brief true-false and multiple-choice test for trustees on basic institutional facts and trends on enrollments, finances, facilities, and programs. Everyone grades their own tests, and no scores are announced, so no one is publicly embarrassed. It is simply this board's way of reminding trustees to stay current and of helping them to see for themselves whether they are in fact doing so.

3

The Interpersonal Dimension

DEFINITION

Competency 3 addresses the **interpersonal dimension,** the development of the board *as a group.* In order to nurture the board's collective welfare and to foster a sense of cohesiveness effective boards: (1) create a sense of inclusiveness among trustees; (2) set goals for themselves; and (3) groom members for leadership positions on the board.

DESCRIPTIONS

A board of trustees is a group. However simple and obvious an observation this may be, many trustees are oblivious to the collective nature, norms, and personality of their board. Thus, the chairman of an ineffective board observed, "We are individual bridges [to various constituencies], we are not some sort of group." And a colleague on the same board confirmed that "we are just an aggregation of individuals who are loyal to the denomination."

The same limitation characterizes corporate boards too. Alderfer (1986, p. 38) noticed "that for the most part directors aren't aware of the group dynamics that affect board behavior." Hence, he identified group dynamics as "the invisible director on corporate boards."

As a genre, boards of trustees have some unusual properties that accentuate the importance of the "invisible director." First, trustees are often drawn from the ranks of corporate executives, senior partners in a professional practice, or other positions at or near the top of an organizational hierarchy. In these roles they customarily have considerable individual authority to act and thus play a more directive role in decision making. Trustees, by comparison, are *peers*. Each trustee's vote carries equal weight in board decisions, and individual trustees rarely have any authority to act formally and independently on the board's behalf. The board *as a group* decides. Moreover, as peers and volunteers, trustees are not as susceptible as inside corporate directors, for example, to pressures to conform to the desires or dictates of management.

Complicating this role, many members of college boards are relative strangers to one another. There are exceptions, of course; a few may be business associates, professional colleagues, or even close friends. Most, however, are not well-acquainted with one another. For boards that are geographically dispersed, this lack of familiarity among trustees may be even more pronounced. Twenty to forty people come together three or four times a year, usually in highly structured meetings on tightly drawn schedules. They discuss the college's affairs, adjourn, and depart. When the board next meets, some members struggle to recall the names of others. Due partially to these circumstances, personal interactions often tend to be formal and superficial, and board discussions are limited and stilted.

All of these conditions affect group dynamics and foster a climate that may strike trustees as rather foreign. To acclimate to such unfamiliar situations and to strengthen the board's collective welfare requires that trustees diligently attend to the "invisible director." Stronger boards do precisely that. In fact, the competency scores on the interpersonal dimension, as assessed by the research team, were 2.5 times greater for the most effective boards as compared to the least effective ones.

When asked to recount a critical incident that illustrated effective trusteeship, members of effective boards by a margin of nearly two to one over trustees of ineffective boards focused on smooth interpersonal relations (Chait, 1989). Indeed, many trustees equated board effectiveness with cohesiveness: "An effective board will be an effective group. Much of the definition of effectiveness will be there in group behavior." This conceptualization of board effectiveness, offered by a trustee of one capable board, was echoed by the current and past chairmen of another strong board:

> The only way to assess effectiveness is that you can see that the board has come together around some common agreements, become less fragmented and more cohesive.

> Effectiveness is a process, a series of inconspicuous things that people do to keep things open, build trust. . . . It's an atmosphere, a set of good relationships that are nurtured over many years.

In contrast, members of weaker boards were more likely to neglect this dimension and to define board effectiveness instead as simply the acquisition of financial and physical resources or the reduction of expenses.

Effective boards relied primarily on three strategies to achieve group solidarity and wholeness:

1. The board creates a sense of inclusiveness among trustees. A group cannot easily develop or sustain unity if even a small minority of its members chronically feel that they are excluded from some inner circle or kept in the dark while others are always "in the know." As might be expected, therefore, among effective boards there was substantially more informal interaction among trustees across diverse settings and more concerted efforts to communicate regularly among all board members.

Too often, trustees are acquainted with one another only as trustees and not, for instance, as dinner companions, tennis partners, or fellow devotees of art, music, theater, and the like. As one midrange board realized, "We need to find the opportunity to spend more time in relaxed discussions. . . . We feel we need to know one another better." Without some even elementary social connections, it is more difficult to learn about and appreciate other facets of a fellow board member's background, personality, and perspectives. Absent these linkages, there are also fewer occasions to accumulate "social credits" or a reservoir of goodwill earned through reciprocal behaviors and common interests that form the basis of mutual trust and respect. Thus, when a fellow trustee known to be thoughtful and considerate at a social or cultural event or on the golf course urges a position in a board meeting, other trustees will be less inclined to attribute that person's behavior to narrow-mindedness or stubbornness. Remembering other positive experiences with this individual, fellow trustees are more likely instead to interpret such behavior as evidence of a deeply held point of view that should be carefully considered.

Mindful of the dividends that accrue from informal interactions among trustees, presidents affiliated with effective boards often created social occasions and opportunities for trustees to become better acquainted. In other words, the president was a crucial supplier of the "social glue" that enabled the board to bond together. As the president of one college with an effective board stated:

> We emphasized participation, commitment, and involvement. My wife and I started having all of the board members and their wives over for dinner, trying to get these folks to know one another outside their formal roles. I've tried to get to know each one personally, to find out about their interest, their strengths, ways they can take on tasks that really interest and involve them.

Another chairman of an effective board touted the benefits of "frequent informal dinners at the president's home or at a trustee's home." On still another campus, rather than have a large dinner for all board members, the college arranged for small groups of trustees to have dinner together at various local restaurants. Smaller dinner groups, the president maintained, were more conducive to social interaction. Finally, other trustees discussed the bonds that form when "we live, eat, and sleep together on the capital campaign trail," when "we travel two hundred miles in school vans once a year to attend a regional conference," when we "get together for dinner at friends' homes," or when "four trustees and their spouses traveled to France together on a university-organized trip."

There are risks, of course, that as some board members, especially local trustees, socialize together at worship, at home, and at the country club, that cliques may form or plots may be hatched. However, none of the presidents or trustees of effective boards whom we interviewed were concerned about any of these possible side effects. Rather they emphasized the informal nature of the events and the personal friendships that were forged. There appeared to be little doubt in their minds that the actual dividends far outweighed the potential drawbacks.

The pleasure that trustees from effective boards derived from social contacts with one another can be contrasted with comments from two members of a decidedly weaker board. The chairman of this board stated flatly: "I'm not a social person, I'm quite private. I'm occasionally invited [to social events] but I've never attended. Some trustees may see each other, but I'm out of the loop. After one or two invitations which I don't accept, people realize that I won't be coming." In similar fashion, a colleague admitted, "I only know one member of the board. I didn't join the board as a means to get to know people." The trustees on this board had distinctly unidimensional and aloof relationships with one another, more strangers than colleagues. Little wonder that their meetings were perfunctory and brief.

Although social relations were important, the flow of information and the patterns of communication within the board were particularly critical variables that affected a trustee's sense of involvement. Just ask the trustee who was "out of the loop" or the board member who complained, "Nobody ever tells me anything." As a longtime trustee of an effective board comprehended:

> Trustees have to learn to trust each other, to be open and involved in the issues. . . . [Otherwise] it is difficult to develop the sort of cohesion and group enthusiasm that is necessary to carry you through difficult problems together. . . . There must be an openness and involvement in the board as a group.

Resolutely committed to broad participation, those in leadership positions on effective boards tried to keep all trustees routinely well-informed. For example, to "equalize information" among the trustees, the chairman of one board meets "with every person between board meetings to go over the issues and their concerns in order to make sure that everyone is informed and heard." At another college, whenever issues arose that required quick board or committee action, the president or chairman arranged a conference call so that distant trustees were included. In addition, this college's president corresponded or spoke with nearly every trustee at least once a month, a practice deeply valued by the board.

> The best thing for our keeping in touch is the president's habit of writing extensively to each of us and calling us on the phone regularly. Sometimes it's to get our advice on an issue he's facing and sometimes it's just to see how we are and to bring us up to date on progress in implementing a decision that the board made at a past meeting. *He makes me feel I'm always an important part of this place.*

Under extraordinary circumstances, effective boards adhered to the same basic approach they employed to communicate about routine events. On crucial or sensitive issues, effective boards were especially careful to keep all board members apprised, whereas at times of crisis less effective boards frequently narrowed or closed the board's channels of communication. Compare, for example, these dramatically different responses to a similar situation: the need to remove the president. In the first instance, most members of one board learned through the press that the executive committee had prompted and accepted the president's resignation. The board as a whole was never consulted, and many trustees were literally speechless when queried by reporters. In the second case, when the board's leadership realized after a year that the new president would not succeed and that other key administrators were poised to resign, the executive committee decided to act. As recounted by the immediate past chairman, his successor first communicated individually "with each member of the board to provide a general review of the situation. He explained that the executive committee had decided to take an action deemed necessary and that the committee needed each board member's understanding and support." Although the need to dismiss a relatively new president was a disappointment to all, the procedure the chairman followed actually drew the board closer together. In the first case, however delicate the circumstances may have been, when trustees learned secondhand about an event of such moment, a sense of distance, detachment, and alienation took hold. Inevitably one started to wonder "How integral am I to the board or the college if I am neither consulted nor apprised of an event as consequential as the president's departure?"

Similar questions may arise if trustees are not encouraged to participate actively in discussions at board and committee meetings. Yet, some less effective boards had clear, even if unstated, norms that limited the number of questions trustees could pose or the length of the discussion the board would abide. One board only convened for about an hour and a half over lunch four or five times a year. "I am impatient," declared the chairman. "We move things quickly. Rather than have endless discussion, we have ninety minutes. We can table things, but I want the business people on the board back in their offices by two P.M. If others want to stay and talk after two, that's fine." When asked about the effects of this pace and procedure on board process, he replied, "My view is, I don't care what happens as long as I get the votes." While awed by the board's efficiency, the president lamented, "If you're lucky, there is a half-hour discussion of key issues." On boards like this one, the norms do not support careful analysis or extended deliberation. Newcomers rapidly learn not to pursue a line of inquiry and not to become deeply involved. Better to call the question than call for additional discussion.

The attitudes and behaviors of effective boards as regards discussion and disagreement differed markedly from the conduct of ineffective boards. As described in chapter 2, the chairs and presidents associated with these stronger boards monitored discussions more closely and actively encouraged widespread participation. For example, one president noted that when topics are debated "I pay attention to the participation and communication of every member, whether people are raising questions and making suggestions. Do they respect one another?" Alderfer (1986, p. 40) noted that one sign of healthy group process was questions and comments that invite response, such as, "Does anybody else feel this way? Am I the only one who is uncomfortable with this? Are we meeting the issue head on?"

> These kinds of comments address the whole group, invite all to share responsibility for shaping the quality of discussion, and discourage blaming individuals when the conversations becomes ridden with conflict. Unless the board develops (and values) a sense of itself as a group, the directors won't ask these questions. From an exclusively individual perspective, they make no sense.

Accordingly, effective boards exhibited more *trustee-to-trustee* or lateral discussions and seldom resorted to a predominantly vertical format where trustees posed questions and the CEO, senior staff, or the chairman responded.

When presidents of colleges with effective boards were asked to explain what most enabled the board to handle a particular event capably, the answer often touched upon the advantageous effects of open and broadly based discussion. Witness these two comments:

> This board has seen itself face and come through some difficult problems. Each person knows his opinion is respected by all the others, that everyone struggles to come to an agreement, makes compromises, but retains the respect of everyone in the group. They believe in themselves individually and as a group.

> We're learning how to allow many opinions to be voiced without becoming panicked and fragmented. We couldn't have done these things in past years.

We would come apart as a board and act just as single individuals. Now we're developing our skills at handling conflict as a group and maintaining our cohesion even during disagreements.

Inclusive and extensive opportunities to cope with a common concern, even where disagreements arose, promoted the board's capacity to coalesce. Engrossed by the issues and entwined by efforts to solve a problem, individuals successfully merged into a group. Conversely, where the norms actively discouraged involvement and engagement, individual trustees drifted apart and toward the periphery since there were no social or intellectual magnets to hold the group together.

2. The board sets goals for itself. Successful teams, whether in management, medicine, athletics, politics, the military, or any other collective endeavor, are typically motivated and united by the pursuit of shared and realistic goals. When these aims are attained (and even when an all-out effort leads to partial success), the group's pride increases and further fortifies a sense of togetherness (Zander, 1982, p. ix).

However familiar trustees of ineffective boards may have been with team play in other walks of life, the idea that a board of trustees might also have some common goals struck many board members as an odd notion. Typical of less effective boards, five of the eight trustees we interviewed on one campus were unable to identify a single goal for their board. Three others mentioned only fund-raising targets. Only one, rather frustrated, trustee perceived the need for some shared objectives. "As a trustee I have no objectives, goals, criteria, or expectations. That's a description, not a preference. . . . I try to make the case for setting goals and criteria, but it never seems to get anywhere." The chairman-designate of another weak board declared, "We have the quantitative goal of one-hundred-percent participation in giving, but we have no qualitative goals." The only goal a fellow trustee could cite was not a board goal at all but rather an "abiding rule of the president" that all trustees be knowledgeable about "what the board is doing." Even on a midrange board a trustee confessed, "I can't think of what a board goal might be."

Members of more effective boards did not have this problem. There was a more explicit commitment to *corporate* accomplishment and a *communal* dedication to the collective aims of the board as a distinctive group. On stronger boards, trustees could more readily delineate board objectives or group goals, defined by Zander (1982, p. 20) as a single product attributable to joint collaboration among the participants.

Some board goals were related to *process*, that is, to actions that would improve the board's ability to function effectively, either internally or in its dealings with critical constituencies. These included, for instance:

To operate smoothly and responsibly as a group.

To be sure we make every opportunity for every board member to get his or her ideas on the table, whether they're reluctant to speak or not.

To be more intimately involved with faculty and students in order to dispel the myth that we're in this for reasons other than serving the college, to become more human in their eyes.

The chairman and leaders of the committees have objectives related to strengthening the capabilities and responsiveness of the board in the areas that need our attention.

Other goals related to *substantive* matters, such as the board's commitment to realize a strategic plan, to complete a development campaign successfully, or to become more knowledgeable about critical aspects of higher education. Stronger boards and presidents worked tirelessly to generate a sense of shared ownership of these larger institutional objectives. As noted earlier, ideas about policy and strategy were openly discussed, debated, and revised by committees and by the board as a whole. When necessary, the board's leadership conferred individually with trustees, not to twist arms or exert pressure but to answer questions and provide information. Even more important, effective boards immersed trustees in the very task at hand and thus engendered a collective commitment through collective involvement. As one president reported about the adoption of a five-year plan:

We had a planning meeting off-campus, which was attended by trustees, administrators, faculty, students, alumni, and a facilitator. We spent a day talking about the college's strengths and weaknesses and about what changes we'd like to make. It was a really free-wheeling discussion. Everyone got inspired by the meeting. . . . Board committees worked through the parts of the plan that affected their areas of responsibility. . . . The idea is to make this the *board's* plan too.

On another campus where the board was heavily involved in an equally extensive process, the president noted that the trustees ultimately internalized the college's goals. "Its goals become their goals. . . . They developed a sense of ownership and responsibility for the goals that emerged."

As related by trustees of effective boards, nearly all of the critical incidents concerning development campaigns stressed a united effort, a collective motivation, and the positive impact of the campaign on the board's self-confidence. To cite only one example, a board chairman recalled:

One of our trustees challenged us with a seven-figure offer for a new student facility if we could match it. Somehow, that mobilized us like nothing else had done. We got on a roll and worked hard to raise the rest. Meeting that challenge seemed to create a level of confidence, an expectation that we were capable of great things together. . . . Most important, we accepted the chal-

lenge and believed we could meet it. We then went into a capital campaign and
drew on all of our contacts and resources. . . . It was a very successful program, one that we can all be proud of. In the process, we developed new
leadership among trustees.

The president there affirmed that "this board knows it can be effective in a
difficult challenge. . . . They believe in themselves, they know they can do
great things for the college."

By comparison, the critical incidents about board goals reported by
members of ineffective boards emphasized *individual* efforts and accentu-
ated the negative effects on the group's self-image. In one case, no trustee we
interviewed could remember an instance where the board as a whole took an
action that made a significant positive difference. "In terms of a total board
effort," the immediate past chairman commented, "I don't know. . . . We
trusted our own individual effectiveness in terms of raising money." However, those efforts were so unsuccessful that for nearly twenty years this
college has been unable to fund a vitally needed laboratory. "We tried and
failed fifteen years ago," the past chairman continued, "and we were scared
we might fail again. . . . A curious number of people avoided me. They knew
I was after them. It was very frustrating." This board of more than thirty
members was not galvanized by any group commitments.

Whatever little this board was able to accomplish was more accurately
due to individual members. The president acknowledged that the board was
not unified by any collective aspirations. "It was basically eight individuals
working with me, and the eight really worked in blocks of one and two.
Most of the action that takes place is with the president and two or three
other board members. They create the agenda and the focus." Hence, the
past chairman accurately ascribed the trustees' failure to raise enough
money for the laboratory to "the board's feeling that the project was foisted
upon them, that they really didn't have ownership over the idea or the
project."

In conclusion, then, effective boards *in consultation with the president*,
set goals for themselves as a group. These aims were not pursued merely for
the sake of "process" but rather as a means to strengthen the board's
internal capacity to contribute constructively to the attainment of another
set of objectives the board embraces, namely, the college's overall aims and
strategic priorities. (Chapter 6 elaborates on the roles of the board and the
president in these endeavors.) The goals served as beacons that guided the
direction of members' efforts and mobilized collaboration among members
(Zander, 1982, p. 114).

**3. The board grooms members for leadership positions on the
board.** Despite the attention we have accorded to the board as group, we
do not mean to suggest that effective boards are self-directed assemblies
without able leaders. To the contrary, we have already noted on several

occasions the critical need for the chairperson and the president most notably to accept responsibility for the board's internal dynamics. Furthermore, effective boards, like any sound corporation, recognized the need to identify and cultivate leaders and to plan for succession *so that the group may thrive.*

Because we were primarily concerned with leadership development within the board, the interviews we conducted did not explore in great depth the nomination and selection process for trustees. Nevertheless, several members of effective boards underscored that leadership development started with a trustee committee that carefully screened candidates with an eye toward "demonstrated leadership skills and potentials."

Even more important, though, effective boards purposively used their trustee committees as an arena to earmark and nurture future board leaders. Since committees are truly the proving ground for prospective leaders, effective boards were more thoughtful about assigning people to committees and more methodical about evaluating their performance, as illustrated by the comments of the past chairman of the board of one college and the president of another:

> The nominating committee, which is composed of the chairs of the various board committees, is very careful to cultivate trustees through various committee assignments. These people have had the opportunity to observe the skills and potentials of their members. We see how they do with committee assignments and then give more responsibility to those who can handle it.

> Our committee on board organization is very careful in its screening of candidates to nominate for the board. . . . Once a person comes aboard, he's assigned to a committee where his skills and interests are needed. The chairman of each committee watches the performance of the members and once a year at least talks to someone on the committee on trusteeship about the performance of committee members. That information is used in developing future assignments and in deciding how a person may best be used in positions of greater responsibility.

Through this process, new leaders emerged to chair committees, to serve as vice chairman and as a member of the executive committee, and eventually to chair the board. On two campuses the chairman and the president worked hand-in-glove for a year with the chairman-designate to prepare that individual for the office and to minimize the slippage during the transition. In one instance this "internship" included attending almost every meeting of the president and the chair.

At the other end of the spectrum, ineffective boards were virtually indifferent to the question of leadership development and succession. Six of the eight trustees we interviewed on one board had no idea how the board cultivated leadership. Another member of that same board observed that "some thought is given to selecting committee chairs so as to groom them for future roles and greater responsibility, but first is a person's ability to give money." On another campus the chairman complained, "I've been telling the board for two years that I can't continue as chairman, and the board's response has been that you have to."

The effects of such apathy were both obvious and substantial. Without a conscious and continuous effort to cultivate leadership, boards were likely to lack leaders, usually sooner rather than later. Under those circumstances, a myriad of problems ensued and trustees' frustrations mounted, as reported by several members of weak boards:

> There is an absence of leadership on the board that has had many bad effects. There is an absence of collegial, cooperative working together and an absence of tolerance.

> What's frustrating? The number of board members who do nothing to aid the college. They just show up.

> At the meeting today there is not really anything for the committees to do.

> There has been little sense of leadership among most members of this board and little feedback about their accomplishments, other than the balance sheet at the end of the fiscal year.

> Actually we have a difficult time recruiting good people onto this board. It was not well led when I joined; I'm not sure it's well led now. They just hit a pop fly and ran it out in recruiting me.

As grave and disturbing as these repercussions were, boards that did not groom leadership faced one other even more severe consequence. While members of boards with a steady flow of leadership expressed confidence in the board's abilities, trustees on less effective boards sounded a note of near desperate and exclusive dependence on the president.

> My biggest fear is losing the president. It is terrifying to be so dependent upon one person. If he resigned we could not run this school. . . . He likes being king of this school. He can get this board to do anything he wants.

> We consider what the president wants us to and very little else. . . . It's a one-man operation.

> I've served under three presidents. Oops, I guess that's a Freudian slip, you know, serving *under* three presidents.

With almost no trustee leadership, these board members were understandably uneasy, without self-confidence, and excessively reliant upon the president—not a comfortable or advisable position. Like nature, a board of trustees should abhor a vacuum, especially a leadership vacuum of its own making.

SUGGESTIONS

An effective board of trustees resembles a successful football team more than a golf foursome, as board members must anticipate and respond to one another's actions and assume different yet related roles. Whereas one golfer's motions are barely affected by the play of others, trustees and football players are part of interdependent teams whose success rests on the capacity of the members to play well as an integral unit. The recommendations offered here are designed to strengthen the board's capacity to function effectively as a group.

Creating a Sense of Inclusiveness

1. ENABLE TRUSTEES TO BECOME BETTER ACQUAINTED WITH ONE AN-OTHER. There are several rather simple steps boards can take not so much to transform relative strangers into close friends as to enable trustees to know one another a little better at a personal level. Rather than breed contempt, familiarity fosters open exchanges and an esprit de corps.

For starters, the board secretary or the president's staff could produce annually a looseleaf notebook that included an up-to-date biographical sketch of each trustee with enough background about each person's experiences, expertise, and interests to help other board members decide who to consult about what issues. In addition, the biographies could list each person's hobbies, pastimes, and travels, information that may help board members discover some common interests—beyond the college—to explore. Including birthdays and anniversary dates offers trustees another opportunity to recognize each other on a personal level.

Second, when the board does meet, an hour or so could be set aside expressly for trustees to interact casually and spontaneously. The board chairman or president should explain the importance and benefits of occasional respites for trustees to become better acquainted, whether through informal conversations, a stroll on campus, a tennis game, or whatever. Frequently, board meetings are so regimented and compressed that no time remains for trustees to become more familiar with one another. That may be efficient in the short run though hardly effective in the long run. Trustees should be encouraged not to look upon "free time" as wasted time.

Third, as we noted earlier, the president and the chairman should take the initiative now and then to organize social events such as dinners, attendance at cultural or athletic events, or participation in educational or recreational activities. Some may coincide with a board meeting and be intended for the entire board, while others may occur between board meetings and involve a subset of trustees. In either case, these gestures by the board's leadership are designed to promote personal and multiple connections among trustees and thereby to buttress the board's capacity to serve and advance the college's welfare.

2. BE SURE EVERYONE UNDERSTANDS THE "RULES OF THE GAME." A senior executive of a Fortune 500 company, by no means an insecure individual, was nonetheless careful to arrive early for his first meeting as a member of the board of directors of another large corporation. The board secretary ushered him into the board room to await his colleagues. Believing that his early arrival would create a favorable impression, the new director sat down, rather pleased with himself, and relaxed until the next director arrived, introduced himself, and promptly announced, "By the way, you're in my seat." "After that," the new director recalled, "my only goal was to get out of there without making a fool of myself." His inadvertent mistake painfully reminded him that he did not know the "rules of the game." Perhaps it was anecdotes like this one that inspired Whisler to write *Rules of the Game: Inside the Corporate Boardroom* (1984), a pithy primer on the "unwritten set of rules" that successful corporate directors voluntarily follow. (See also Mueller, *Behind the Boardroom Door*, 1984.)

The boards of colleges, universities, and other nonprofits for that matter also have unspoken norms and unwritten rules that are important to understand. (Some are described in chapter 4.) Just as effective boards share institutional information widely to create a climate of inclusiveness, so too should boards share widely information about important organizational norms. For example, newcomers to a board typically wonder: Is it acceptable here to disagree openly with the CEO? With the chair of the board? Is it "permissible" to question or to vote against a committee recommendation? Does the board tolerate an extended line of inquiry by an individual trustee? How do these trustees handle grapevine information? Is it okay to arrive late, leave early, or miss a board meeting?

In order to truly feel a part of the group, trustees need to know the answer to questions such as these. Board members unaware of the group's customs and conventions are more apt to participate tentatively, to blunder inadvertently, and to feel outside the circle. On the other hand, newcomers would probably be more comfortable and more productive sooner were the "rules of the game" explained early. When we asked, trustees of effective boards, in fact, were readily able to cite crucial yet tacit guidelines. For example:

> We don't rely heavily on rules of order, unless it's a very difficult issue. . . . Don't hesitate to speak up, raise questions, probe for the reasons behind a recommendation, propose alternatives, then move on.

Provide support for the president. Don't try to order him to do things, use persuasion, not control, be a team player, not a solo achiever.

Support the president when he has good ideas, and offer suggestions when he doesn't.

Even members of ineffective boards sometimes had "helpful" advice to acclimate newcomers. To wit, one trustee said, "We are a supportive board. We are not going to say to the president, 'That's B.S.' There's a lot of deference, a readiness to do whatever's recommended." Irrespective of the wisdom of such counsel, it *is* information a new member of this board would be well-advised to have.

How might the unspoken code of conduct be transmitted? Newcomers might be paired with one or more mentors or coaches. These sympathetic and experienced trustees could communicate informally and tactfully the board's key norms, as well as answer any questions about the board's operations that a recently appointed trustee might be reluctant to ask in a group setting. Behavioral expectations could also be addressed diplomatically by the board chairperson and by the college president as part of an orientation program. Other less sensitive procedural matters, such as attendance requirements, classroom visitations, or communications with the press, could be incorporated into a trustee handbook. Unless such efforts are undertaken, board members will have to learn the rules by observation over time, a very uneven and sometimes awkward or hurtful process that slows assimilation and effective participation.

Once in a while, even experienced trustees may be uncertain or confused about an aspect of the board's informal code of conduct. There may be a perception, for instance, that some board members violated what other board members believed to be a group norm. Maybe the rules have changed, should change, or need clarification. Whatever the case, boards might schedule now and then a question and answer period where trustees at an executive session or a retreat can ask directly or anonymously (e.g., on an index card) "What I've always wanted to know about how we operate as a board, but I was afraid to ask." As a result of this process, board members will be better informed about the group's unwritten rules, they will feel more like a member of the team, and they will probably perform more effectively.

Setting Group Goals

1. GENERATE COMMITMENT TO THE BOARD'S GOALS. We have already observed that an effective board, in concert with the college's president, sets both process-oriented and substantive goals *for the board.* But just to establish goals is not enough; the board must also be committed to achieving them. How does a board strengthen commitment to a particular objective?

Citing an earlier study by Salancik, Goodman and Dean (1982, p. 270) noted that "the level of commitment is highest when the adopted behavior is: (1) selected freely (not because it is an organizational requirement), (2) explicit (that is, not easily deniable), and (3) publicly known."

To translate this model into concrete terms, consider a common, personal goal: to lose weight. While the advice of a physician or an article on fitness may lead someone to start a weight-loss program, the commitment to persevere ultimately depends upon an individual's determination to be healthier or trimmer. Once that decision has been made, some dieters post next to the scale or on a refrigerator or closet door a chart that measures their progress toward a stated (i.e., "not easily deniable") goal. And people really committed to losing weight openly proclaim the target to relatives or friends and attend a weekly weigh-in with other dieters, where the goals are "publicly known" and publicly monitored. How much weaker the commitment would be if an individual were only to muse silently that "I need to lose some weight," but did not specify an explicit goal or tell another soul.

The model applies equally well to a board's goals. To increase trustees' commitment to some collective aims, the board's goals should be thoroughly discussed, clearly developed, and voluntarily embraced by the board and the president, perhaps at a retreat or as part of an annual self-study. To be explicit and not "easily deniable," the goals should be unambiguously memorialized through a resolution or as a part of the board's minutes. As a result, there would be a greater sense of ownership and a stronger recognition that the board's self-esteem was at stake. The commitment could not be very easily eluded by selective recall or artful reinterpretation, because the board's goals would be "on the record." Finally, while there may be some exceptions related to confidentiality or competitive strategy, the board's goals should be publicized across the campus community. This step not only heightens the board's own commitment, but dissemination may also: (1) correct any misperceptions on- or off-campus about the board's aims, (2) alter any impressions that the board feels no responsibility to communicate its priorities to the campus at large, and (3) elicit some constructive suggestions to help the board achieve its objectives. The plain fact is that on many campuses only a few people have even the faintest notion of the board's roles, responsibilities, and priorities. Distributing its goals may help the board remedy this situation.

2. *CHOOSE REALISTIC GOALS.* Without a "psychological bond" (O'Reilly, 1989, p. 295) to a particular objective, trustees are, of course, less likely to achieve that goal. And as we explained in chapter 2, absent regular and accurate information about the board's performance to date, trustees can all too easily develop unrealistic goals, a problem that affects other groups as well. "Without reliable evidence about the group's progress, members tend to think their group is highly productive even when it is not and tend to prefer goals typically chosen by successful groups" (Zander, 1982, p. 115). Ironi-

cally, boards that fail to attain a stated aim are more likely than successful boards to select subsequently even more unreasonable targets. Apparently with each setback, unsuccessful boards become more concerned with the need to avoid further public humiliation and loss of esteem. These needs supersede any tendency to set sensible levels of achievement. Such groups "perceive that a failure on a difficult goal is less embarrassing than a failure on an easy goal and they therefore choose an unreasonably difficult goal" (Zander et al., 1969, p. 74).

To avoid the spiral of increasingly unreasonable goals, boards of trustees should: (1) resist vague, global aspirations such as to serve humankind or to create the nation's finest college; (2) review prior performance levels on similar objectives; (3) regularly receive factual feedback on progress to date; (4) encourage comparisons with other boards that have set comparable goals; and (5) invite constituent groups and most especially the president to suggest priorities and to articulate realistic expectations of the board. And when the board realizes a goal, remember that groups, like individuals, need to recognize and celebrate their accomplishments.

Grooming Leadership

1. DEVELOP A "FARM SYSTEM." In order to become better informed about a prospective trustee's potential, a few boards have established a "farm system" where possible board members are first asked to serve on alumni councils, visiting committees, college task forces, or board committees. As one board chairman explained about an advisory council, "We do watch the council to identify people who may become more broadly interested in the college and able to work with the board at a higher level. So it also serves as a grooming process for good new trustees." By the same token, these experiences afford potential trustees the opportunity to learn more about the college and the board and to decide more knowledgeably whether to accept an appointment to the board should one be offered. A trustee from such a farm system has a "head start" and thus may become an effective participant on the board a little sooner than other, less prepared newcomers. Lastly, advisory boards, task forces, and similar structures offer a way to draw upon a larger talent pool and to match tasks and skills without expanding the size of the board.

2. ESTABLISH INFORMAL "GROWTH CONTRACTS" WITH TRUSTEES. Board leaders need to be well-informed about the essence of academe, the subtleties of governance, and the multiple dimensions of the board's role in the institution. In part, trustees gain that expertise through mentors, retreats, educational materials, and service on various committees. Still some gaps may remain. A simple way to reduce these gaps would be for the committee on trusteeship to ask all board members once a year or so to identify the areas where they wanted to become more knowledgeable. The "trustee audit," developed by AGB as part of its *Self-study Guidelines* to help board members assess "the extent to which they have absorbed the breadth and depth of their roles and institutions" (Association of Governing Boards, 1986), could easily be adapted to serve this purpose.

Based on board members' responses to such a questionnaire, informal, voluntary, and uncomplicated trustee-development plans could be formulated. While useful for all board members, the target population should include committee chairs and vice-chairs, members of the executive committee, or trustees flagged as leaders by incumbent board officers and the president. The development plan for these likely leaders might include, for example, a visit with trustees in similar positions at comparable institutions, attending a specialized workshop or seminar, or being "tutored" for a day by the appropriate senior staff member. Such activities enable the board *systematically* to groom board leaders through a deliberate trustee development program.

DISCUSSION QUESTIONS AND EXERCISES

1. Do we know one another well enough to have conversations about common interests that extend beyond the college? Do board members have personal as well as collegial relationships with one another? If not, set aside fifteen minutes or so at each board meeting for a few trustees to talk briefly about why they joined the board and to share some information about themselves not on their official college biographies.

2. Do board members at least occasionally interact with each other at social, recreational, or cultural events? If not, are there any events or activities the board could initiate that would increase social interactions among trustees, yet not seem to be too contrived?

3. Ask each trustee to list (1) what are and (2) what should be the two or three most important goals *of the board*. Collate each list to determine the degree of consensus. Can a set of priorities for the board's further development be agreed upon? What evidence would best indicate that these goals have been achieved? How should the board's progress toward these ends be monitored? To what extent should the board publicly disclose its goals?

4. Who bears primary responsibility for ensuring that the board has adequate leadership in the years ahead? Does the board have a plan to groom prospective leaders? If not, what realistic and immediate steps can the board take to start the process?

4

The Analytical Dimension

DEFINITION

Competency 4 addresses a board's **analytical skills**, its capacity to dissect complex problems and to draw upon multiple perspectives to synthesize appropriate responses. Effective boards approach problems from a broad institutional outlook, search widely for information, and actively seek different points of view. Aware of the subtleties and nuances of multifaceted issues, effective boards tolerate ambiguity and recognize that complex matters rarely yield to perfect solutions.

DESCRIPTIONS

The board views events through several different "lenses."

More than any of the five other dimensions of effective trusteeship, the analytical component concerns a rather abstract notion: cognition, or how people perceive, think, and know. Fortunately, however, a few studies of leadership have plainly articulated the central concepts, and several questions we posed to trustees elicited responses that illustrated quite concretely the cognitive differences between effective and ineffective boards.

Bolman and Deal (1986, pp. 2–7) posited that the vast literature on organizational theory could be condensed into four schools of thought about different ways to conceptualize organizations. In brief, these models are as follows:

Rational systems models assume that organizations exist to accomplish stated goals. To do so requires clear roles, bureaucratic structures, rules and regulations, and a chain of command.

Human resource models assume that institutions exist to serve human needs. The organization relies less on supervision and control and more on creating an environment where people can realize their potential and capitalize on self-motivation.

Political models view institutions as structured around the reality of scarce resources. Organizations are coalitions of interest groups that bargain to set goals and reach decisions. Power, conflict, and negotiation are central features of organizational life.

Symbolic models emphasize the importance of the interpretation people attach to events rather than the decisions or actions themselves. Organizations are drama and theater. Beliefs, culture, rituals, ceremonies, myths, and metaphors provide meaning and make confusion comprehensible.

These theories, termed "frames" by Bolman and Deal (p. 4), provide lenses or perspectives that managers use to gather information, reach decisions, and take actions. "Frames are windows on the world. Frames filter out some things while allowing others to pass through easily. Frames help us to order the world . . . "

To quibble about the number or description of these frames would be to miss the central point: where and how we look determines what we see.[1] If a trustee were to view a college (or an executive were to view a corporation) through only one of these frames, some facets of a problem would be sharply illuminated, while other aspects would be blurred or even invisible.

Taken alone, each frame sheds light on only a part of the problem at hand. Thus, Bolman and Deal recommended that executives analyze important issues through all four lenses. When problems are diagnosed in that way, people will be much better able to understand events and reactions, to develop successful change strategies, to better predict outcomes, and to avoid surprises. In short, multiple lenses enable people to be better managers and leaders, a conclusion corroborated in a study of college presidents by Bensimon et al. (1989, p. 72).

> The difference between effective and ineffective leaders may be related to cognitive complexity. It has been suggested that academic organizations have multiple realities and that leaders with the capacity to use multiple lenses are likely to be more effective than those who analyze and act on every problem

---

[1] In *Essence of Decision* (1971), Allison offers an incisive analysis of the Cuban missile crisis and the consequences of overreliance by policymakers on the "Rational Actor or 'Classical' Model" as their conceptual framework.

using a single perspective. If they are to be effective, academic leaders must recognize the interactions between the bureaucratic, collegial, political, and symbolic processes present in all colleges and universities at all times.

The same could be said of boards of trustees. That is, effective trustees realized that most policy questions before the board were complicated, many-sided issues that needed to be examined from several perspectives. Recall, for example, the incident described in chapter 1 where a board of trustees voted to eliminate the college's astronomy program. From a *rational* perspective, the appropriate course of action seemed obvious: terminate the program. "This was a financial matter, a bottom line decision," one trustee remarked. Yet, there was a pronounced outcry from alumni concerned that one of the college's most distinctive and historic programs would be abolished and from professors concerned about the fate of the program faculty.[2] If the board had not ignored these political, symbolic, and humanistic elements of the equation, a more creative solution might have emerged and, even if not, trustee attention to the viewpoints of others would have had a positive influence on these constituencies.

To cite another example, one ineffective board responded solely from a bureaucratic perspective to a perceived crisis with respect to administrative incompetence. The board defined the problem narrowly as financial mismanagement and the solution was to place the college in effect under the receivership of the finance committee of the board. In short order the board assumed command.

> We had the skills, and the need was clearly there. A lot of the funds that were coming to the college were not controlled by the board. The new policy said that the board must be involved. We wanted to get control of the college again. Now, at each board meeting, each committee meets with appropriate administrators for an hour and a half to communicate and to direct the administration to act.

A splendid solution, *unless* one were concerned about faculty morale, staff motivation, the symbolism of a trustee "takeover," and the intensification of political strife on campus. In other words, the board's response was perfectly "rational" from one perspective yet far from perfect from several other perspectives.

When viewed only through one frame, trustees may see a simple, uncomplicated world. "The issues we face," commented the past chairman of one ineffective board, "are straightforward. Finances control all of our decisions these days. When you have money, you can do lots of nice things." True

---

[2] Coca-Cola made a similar miscalculation about the power of symbols and emotions when the board of directors discontinued "Classic" Coke. The product was reinstated, of course, but only after the company realized that Coke in its original formula was more than a drink; it was also a treasured part of America's culture.

enough, except that money alone cannot solve all of any college's problems (Chaffee, 1984). When a board sees every question of policy, strategy, and purpose as "straightforward," there's a strong probability that those trustees have not analyzed the issue through more than one lens.

Effective boards perceived a more intricate web and appreciated that an issue may, for instance, be both political and procedural, or symbolic as well as structural, and not merely one or the other. Emotionally charged, complex issues such as divestment were not approached simply as a matter of investment policy or solely as questions of conscience and values. Competent boards were more inclined to think "both/and" rather than "either/or," and to describe board actions with multiple objectives derived from the use of multiple frames.

Thus, on one campus when faculty dissatisfaction over salaries started to simmer, the finance committee, the president, and the board chairman collectively determined that the college had to deal with the inextricably linked financial, political, and educational dimensions of the situation. Among the board's goals, as reported by a senior trustee, were "to offer modest raises, develop better communication with the faculty about the college's financial condition, and to defuse the tension and restore trust." Not every board (and not every administrator) would understand and address the interrelated aspects of such a policy decision. Indeed, for many trustees faculty salaries were a simple matter of economics and managerial prerogatives.

To provide another set of examples of limited cognitive complexity, less effective boards tended to regard communication with various constituencies essentially through one frame as "good politics" or astute internal public relations. While the political calculus was undoubtedly important, weaker boards rarely acknowledged the highly symbolic content of many forms of communication. More effective boards did. Meeting with faculty and students about the selection of a new president was a "way for the board to take its place in the community," to recall a critical incident cited earlier. This same board organized a meeting with students to discuss divestment in a session co-chaired by a student and a trustee, with everyone seated in a semicircle around a fireplace in the student center. Such an approach conveyed definite values and signaled clearly an openness to a free exchange of views. And, on a slightly more conceptual level, the past chairman of another effective board observed that while communication "is basic to governance, that communication must be *celebrative* as well as factual." There needed to be heroes and ceremonies, "people need to be recognized," and the college "needs to celebrate its successes in reaching its goals and serving its mission." Mindful of the symbolic as well as the political frame, these boards were able to communicate more sensitively and more eloquently with their constituents.

In sum, when a board views governance through different lenses, the world of trusteeship ironically becomes both more complicated and better illuminated. Multiple frames expand a board's peripheral vision and its depth perception, thereby affording trustees a broader and sharper panorama of the organizational landscape. Hence, trustees are less likely to see a problem as "just" a matter of structure, politics, or symbols. With multiple frames, there are more vantage points and trade-offs to consider. The additional information can temporarily complicate a board's deliberations, yet with thoughtful discussion the component parts eventually make sense as a whole precisely because the board took the time and care to survey a problem from numerous vantage points.

The board perceives subtlety and nuance.

Concepts such as subtlety and nuance are not easily captured, let alone measured. Nevertheless we observed that with a few exceptions trustees of effective boards offered deeper and subtler responses than members of less effective boards to some deceptively simple questions about a trustee's role, the president's role, and advice to a newcomer on the board.

One set of questions invited interviewees to reflect on the unique aspects of a trustee's role "at this college as compared with other roles you play in your professional or public life." Respectively the past chairman and a trustee of one effective board and the current chairman and a trustee of another equally effective board responded as follows:

A trustee is not an executive or a manager. As a manager, I make my own decisions day to day and insist on specific actions from my staff. But as a trustee, I work as part of a group, and together we deal with the overall directions of the total organization. . . . We act as a group, not as individuals.

The role of trustee seems larger, broader in its responsibilities, not so limited or specific in focus. The board has to be aware of the total system, not just a part that I may be interested in. Not that we are to get directly involved in things, but we must know about what goes on in all areas of the system, how one thing affects another.

As a trustee, I don't have to deal with daily administrative responsibilities for the organization, like I have to do in my corporation. The role of trustee is broader than that of an executive and not restricted to any one area or aspect of the organization. It involves looking at trends in the environment and needs of the total college. From these considerations, we develop advice for the president, guidelines for his activities and day-to-day efforts in running the college.

In my management position in my firm, I make daily administrative decisions and give specific assignments to my staff. Here, I'm more like a shareholder than a proprietor. I'm probably something of an autocrat at work. . . . Here, it's essential that I am a team member and participate in the group process.

These four respondents sounded several common themes that reflect an awareness of some distinctive aspects of a trustee's role. Trustees are *members of a group* that adopts a *broad institutional perspective* and *exercises limited authority, often influencing events indirectly.* The comments also conveyed an appreciation for subtlety, such as the need to be informed though not overly involved, and for complexity, such as the need to relate the parts to the whole.

Confronted with the same question about the trustee's unique role, several members of ineffective boards had no answer. Others offered only superficial responses. "The different role of a trustee? It is not in my home community. It requires me to be away." And still others could see no difference. "It's not unique from being a church leader." Or "I'll be honest and tell you that being a trustee carries the same responsibility as being on the board of my company or any other board. You represent the shareholders and have to be committed. The only difference is that I consider this my service to the church." The "secret" to service on any board, declared another trustee, is to "show up, prepare, and work."

Notice that these comments evidenced no awareness of the trustee's relationships with the president and other board members, little appreciation for the trustee's special and collective responsibilities, and no sensitivity to the nature of a trustee's power and influence. When compared to the responses from effective boards, these observations therefore seem shallow and cursory. There was little or no analysis, never mind profundity.

Similar patterns were observed when trustees addressed the president's role. Members of less effective boards articulated a narrower and sometimes simplistic conceptualization of the president and the CEO's relationship to the board. There was naivete at both extremes, whether the president was viewed as "the king: so goes the president, so goes the board," or, at the other end, where the president was regarded as little more than the board's hired agent. "The board sets policy and directions and tries to pick somebody who can implement them. A weak president tends to draw the board into administrative issues. Such a person should go. The board made a mistake." For one chairman, the intricacies of the presidency could all be reduced to one word, "accountability," and to one document, "a clearly defined position description," that specified the president's functions and the board's functions. "That's the key." No more was needed.

In reality, though, college presidencies are very complex positions not easily encapsulated by any catchphrase or static position description. Matters of context, style, vision, values, behaviors, and constituent relations—all crucial elements of the success or failure of a presidency—are rarely delineated in position descriptions. Members of effective boards demonstrated a greater understanding of the inherently dynamic and multidimensional nature of the president's position, as the following comments illustrate.

A college changes by evolution, not by executive order. The president seems more like a sort of referee or coach, keeping the game in bounds and offering suggestions for improving the plays, but not demanding a specific formation. All of the participants—the students, the faculty, the staff, even the board— need to be stimulated and challenged to do their best with the issues they face and the resources available to them and to do so in some partial awareness of what the other groups are also doing. Balancing all these multiple interests with cajoling and persuasion is a fine art. I really admire how well the president manages all that.

The president has many hats to wear. It is a terribly demanding position. He has to juggle a lot of balls. . . . The president must set examples: moral examples, leadership examples, discipline must be exacted, expectations set. It requires the ability to recruit and keep people, the ability to keep constituents reasonably happy and sustain a common goal, to carry out the mission.

Again, when compared with the observations of trustees on weaker boards, these descriptions by members of better boards are subtler, more textured, and more attuned to the many nuances of the presidency. Rather than attempt to simplify a complex administrative position, these trustees recognized the complications that limit the value of any bromides about the presidency.

The third question we raised that provided a way to gauge a board's analytical strengths concerned what advice a trustee would offer to a newcomer to the board. Specifically, we asked, "Is there any unwritten or unspoken information that new trustees should have in order to be effective members of this board?" Tacitly the question invited trustees to analyze their group's norms and operating style and to think about what was required to be a constructive participant.

Consistent with reactions to the other questions, "I don't know" was a very common response among members of less effective boards. Even when explicitly prompted to discuss an important unwritten rule or an unspoken norm, many trustees still seemed baffled. "We don't have any unwritten rules. If it's not on the table, we don't deal with it." "I don't know that we have any unwritten rules. I always try to keep everything on the table and cut through the B.S." "I can't think of anything, unless they started eating with their toes or, by next year, maybe smoking at board meetings."

A second set of responses, mostly from trustees on midrange boards, did answer the question, although not with any particular insight or sophisticated analysis. "Don't talk about problems outside of meetings." "Contribute time, expertise, and money." "Don't say dumb things." Essentially these trustees offered glib advice not likely to be unknown or especially helpful to a newcomer. Certainly none of the comments suggested an astute observer.

Trustees of the most effective boards consistently volunteered responses that were notably more perceptive and would be truly useful to a newcomer. Even their mundane advice had a little more contour and nuance. Thus, where a midrange trustee recommended "contribute time, expertise, and money," a member of a more effective board added some important, subtle details (underlined). "Provide financial support *within your means*; give your skills, your time, your talents *to help the college grow.*"

The most astute comments were even more attentive to roles, relationships, the board's culture, and a newcomer's likely concerns. Thus, on one especially effective board the counsel offered to a newcomer included:

> Remember that the board as a group comes to decisions, not you as an individual. . . . Never undercut the board or the president by your words or actions. . . . Get to know well any of your fellow trustees that you don't already know, build trust and confidence with them. Learn how to disagree forcefully on issues, without being disagreeable personally.
>
> Avoid factions and win-lose struggles that polarize. At the same time, don't be afraid to challenge ideas and demand that strong reasons are given for any recommendations.
>
> Find out the issues and the influences behind them, seek alternatives and options. . . . Watch what succeeds and what doesn't, so you can learn from your mistakes.

Such advice from members of an effective board to new trustees reflected a more incisive analysis of the board's "personality" and deeper insight into the needs and concerns of newcomers. The topics—interpersonal relations, group dynamics, the norms of participation—and the patterns of thought tended to be more complex and more intricate than the counsel offered by trustees of less effective boards. In a word, effective boards were more analytical.

The board tolerates ambiguity, pursues information, and encourages debate.

Tolerating Ambiguity. In a seminal study of the college presidency, Cohen and March (1974, pp. 195–203) observed that college presidents face four fundamental ambiguities: the ambiguity of power, purpose, experience, and success. No one is quite sure who is in charge, toward what ends, what exactly should be learned from past performance, or what defines personal or institutional achievement. While some critics contend that the authors overstated the case, the essence of Cohen and March's argument nonetheless holds true: colleges and universities are awash in ambiguities. For trustees accustomed to working in environments with clear lines of authority, a singleminded commitment to profitability, and the precise yardstick of the bottom line, the ambiguities of academe can quickly generate frustration and tempt trustees to superimpose a business model, as noted in chapter 1.

People uncomfortable with ambiguity prefer that issues be packaged as "clear cut" or "black and white." Imperfect solutions, trade-offs, and shades of gray are not especially appreciated. Often these individuals prescribe favored remedies irrespective of context, circumstances, or contingencies. For instance, one trustee of an ineffectual board categorically asserted that "decisiveness is effectiveness," although one could readily imagine situations where delay and doubt on a board's part would be advisable. An intolerance for ambiguity also leads people to espouse absolute canons such as "the board always sets policy, the administration only implements policy." These attitudes toward rules are consistent with Berliner's (1989) research on the differences between novices and experts. With little experience or expertise, the former are overly reliant on rules while the latter have learned that rules frequently need to be modified or even disregarded in some circumstances.

More effective boards appeared to be less troubled by ambiguity and compromise. When a faculty member, on sabbatical at another college, accepted an offer to remain there rather than return to his home campus for a year, as institutional policy required, some trustees were upset. The board could easily have decided to sue since this professor had breached college policy. On some boards this would have been an open-and-shut case. Instead, the president in this case reported:

> There were folks on all sides of the issue, and the discussions were spirited and candid. . . . They agreed that it was important that they come to a conclusion that everyone could live with. They accepted that there was no perfect solution and that compromises would have to be made by everyone. . . . In the end they demanded that he pay some nominal sum, a few thousand dollars. But the point is that they examined all sides of the problem in order to work out a conclusion that allowed everyone to retain parts of what they believed to be important.

The president played an instrumental role, talking with trustees individually and together to help them understand that there was no obvious or ideal solution. Every alternative had both positive and negative implications for campus governance and faculty morale, and all of the options were considered and integrated into a final conclusion.

In a situation on another campus that involved a controversy over intercollegiate athletics, the board wrestled at great length with various flawed "solutions." Eventually, the board concluded that "there's just no clear answer to a problem like this." Resigned that "some issues are just no-win situations," the board decided against any dramatic changes and vowed instead to pay careful attention to the issue and to remain well-informed, a reasonable response under the circumstances. A board uneasy with ambiguity might have forced the question and adopted a new "solution" which in turn would have created new problems.

Pursuing Information. We do not mean to suggest that effective boards did not take action. In fact, when confronted with ambiguities, better boards did act and their first step usually entailed an active search for additional information, a measure less effective boards sometimes bypassed or curtailed en route to a speedy decision.

In *The Change Masters*, Kanter (1983, p. 27) characterizes the problem-solving techniques of innovative, entrepreneurial corporations as "integrative: the willingness to move beyond received wisdom, to combine ideas from unconnected sources." In order to promote ingenuity, these organizations broadly conceptualize rather than disaggregate problems and then "create mechanisms for exchange of information and new ideas across organizational units (and) ensure that multiple perspectives will be taken into account in decisions." Conversely, less inventive companies assumed "that problems can be solved when they are carved into pieces and the pieces assigned to specialists who work in isolation." Such "segmentalist" companies defined problems from a narrow perspective, compartmentalized departments, and limited exchanges across the internal boundaries of the organization.

The behaviors of the boards of trustees we studied present a similar pattern. With the president's encouragement and concurrence, effective boards regularly crossed organizational boundaries to engage key constituencies— faculty, students, staff, and alumni—in focused discussions of specific policies, problems, and priorities. Thus, the president affiliated with a most effective board urged trustees to "be quite familiar with the campus, students, faculty, staff, the curriculum, the buildings, and facilities."

The avenues for such inquiry, which varied from campus to campus and from issue to issue, included joint task forces, open forums, and direct conversations with faculty and students. On one campus the student members of the board's college-life committee recommended and conducted a poll of students to assess the acceptability of an increase in activity fees as a means to finance more on campus entertainment. Because these various discussions were focused and arranged after consultation with the president, no one was apprehensive about "end runs" or violating the "chain of command," concerns that were often raised by CEOs and trustees of less effective boards.

In the next chapter, we elaborate upon the structural mechanisms and political benefits of consultation with constituencies. Here we want to emphasize a more fundamental point: effective boards initiated these "integrative" conversations as a way to augment the intellectual horsepower of the discussion and to improve the quality of the ideas on the table. These goals were perhaps best exemplified by the format of a retreat, designed by an especially effective board and president, to consider the college's priorities for a capital campaign.

The most useful action was to break the board at the retreat into four small groups with fluid membership. There was always faculty and administrative expertise present in each group. The groups were initially composed to have different points of view so not everyone thought alike just to build a quick consensus. The groups, which lasted about an hour each, were shuffled. Different groups would be constituted to look at the same topical areas like facilities, academics, and endowment. The degree of interaction between the board, faculty, and administration was what made the retreat effective. . . . There were subtle shifts in priority by the board; individual trustees contributed substantively to the discussion. They thought of things others had not thought of.

This board searched for "dissensus" before arriving at consensus (Birnbaum, 1988, p. 216). Its retreat was deliberately structured to encourage dissent within a group as a way to proliferate ideas and to detect and correct possible errors of judgment. The design permeated organizational boundaries and actually *invited* participants to surface conflicts of opinion, a situation ineffective boards preferred to avoid, as we illustrate shortly.

The search for information sometimes extended well beyond the board and the campus. When faced with decisions about divestment, for instance, two effective boards established special committees to learn as much as possible about the issue through conversations with scholars, South Africans in the United States, corporate officials, and advocates on both sides of the question. Another board's committees routinely drew on outsiders, "anyone who is knowledgeable about matters we're working on. That makes for better ideas and sounder conclusions to bring to the board, and it expands involvement and the sense of participation in the college on the part of more people." These actions might be compared with the response of a board that was poised to discontinue an academic program. One officer of the board recalled, "I received about sixty or seventy letters to overturn the upcoming decision. There was no effort to identify a specific board group to become fully informed on this. . . . We didn't invite anyone to speak. The alumni view was represented by the alumni on the board."

And therein lies the difference. Effective boards eagerly sought information from disparate sources likely to have diverse points of view. Ineffective boards did not. For better boards, additional information and differences of opinion provided the intellectual resources and energy to explore alternatives and synthesize options. For ineffective boards, more information and different viewpoints more often than not only confused matters. Not surprisingly, these attitudes extended to the value of hearty debate.

Encouraging Debate. In the previous chapter, we observed that effective boards endeavored to have inclusive discussions and "lateral" conversations among trustees. Here we stress a related yet different feature: effective boards encouraged lively debate as well as broad participation. There were few efforts to limit debate, rush toward a consensus, or squelch dissent. Quite the opposite, respectful disagreement was regarded as a positive, even essential, component of a productive discussion.

The pronounced differences between effective and ineffective boards on this score were clearly discernible in some of the advice trustees would offer to newcomers. Some members of less capable boards were remarkably frank about the board's distaste for debate and disagreement. One such trustee warned,

> Bring all your company manners and a comfortable cushion, since board meetings are really just social hours. Avoid confronting anyone or insisting on decisions, since you'll just frustrate yourself and embarrass everyone else who's there for a good time. Keep your expectations low and your thoughts to yourself, and you'll get along just fine.

On a less cynical yet equally candid note, a trustee of a midrange board offered similar counsel. "Don't be too critical; we don't handle it well. Don't ever recommend dropping football, and don't criticize the alumni association. We are a supportive board." Mindful that the board does not want to raise "very sensitive, controversial issues," the newly installed president on this campus has attempted to change the board's behavior. "I asked for executive sessions at each board meeting to get more discussion and I told them I wanted more discussion." This goal may be realized, since the president has a powerful influence over the substance and character of board discussions. To underscore the president's central role in shaping the tenor of the board's deliberations, we quote Alderfer (1986, p. 42):

> CEOs set the style of board-management exchanges by the kinds of issues they bring to the board, by the quality and timeliness of the information they give directors, by the nature of their presentations, and perhaps most important, by their responses to board members' discerning questions.

> CEOs also affect the board's group dynamics by the kinds of issues they take up with directors individually and then do not bring forward for the whole board to consider. The more a CEO indicates to directors that they should discuss sensitive issues outside the boardroom, the more members will remain silent when these kinds of topics come up and the less the board will develop a sophisticated capacity to work as a group with such subjects.

Further evidence of the president's influence can be seen at a college where the CEO urged trustees "not to be afraid to challenge ideas and demand that strong reasons are given for any recommendation." Not coincidentally, the advice that members of this board would offer to novices on the board carried the same refrain.

> Don't be hesitant to raise your concerns, say what you really think, ask questions and raise objections to others' ideas when you think they are weak or inadequate. At the same time, be prepared to give good grounds or reasons for your concerns. Don't just pop off without thinking.

Challenge issues and push for excellence. We're not hesitant to debate and to do so quite vigorously. Everybody gets his say and no one is afraid to challenge another. But after we challenge everything and push it to the limit, we come to one conclusion we can all support.

Favorably disposed toward open exchange and spirited debate, effective boards were less apt to whisk through an agenda and applaud the board's efficiency or to passively accept committee and administrative reports and applaud everyone's perspicacity. Instead, trustees on competent boards realized that forthright discussions were necessary to "find out the issues and the influences behind them," "to seek alternatives and options," "to raise questions and to probe the reasons behind a recommendation," and "to challenge ideas . . . and not settle for what is convenient or easy."

SUGGESTIONS

It is not easy for trustees, or anyone else for that matter, to suddenly become "more analytical." From a president's perspective, a simpler course might be to recruit "brighter" trustees and, likewise, trustees may prefer to recruit a "smarter" president. These options, however, are not always available and, in any event, the mere presence of intelligent people does not guarantee that the board and the president together will be more analytical. Furthermore, there are specific and concrete measures boards can adopt that foster cognitive complexity and analytical thinking. These techniques have one common purpose: to create an environment conducive to open discussion and consideration of all sides of the question at hand.

Put another way, these mechanism are designed to reduce the possibility that boards of trustees fall prey to the perils of "groupthink," where all or nearly all members of the board fasten onto the same perspective viewed through the same single frame. Janis (1972, p. 9) defined groupthink as "a mode of thinking that people engage in when they are deeply involved in a cohesive in-group, when the members' strivings for unanimity override their motivation to realistically appraise alternative courses of action." As a consequence, such a board: (1) considers few or no alternative definitions of the problem or the solution; (2) discounts or disregards advice and information contrary to the consensus; (3) overlooks the downside of the preferred plan of action; and (4) rarely formulates contingency plans "just in case we're wrong." What then can a board do to be "more analytical?"

Use Multiple Frames to Analyze Issues and Events. We have already commended the practice of viewing situations through multiple lenses. Since that does not typically occur naturally, we suggest that boards develop and institutionalize the process. When confronted with a proposal for a new degree program, most boards have a regimen or line of inquiry that includes basic questions about the financial, physical, academic, and marketplace implications. Similarly, when presented with a policy recommendation, the board could assess the proposal and the likely consequences through a series of questions that reflect respectively the rational, political, symbolic, and human resource frames. As an example, if a merit pay plan were under consideration, the board might ask: Do we have the funds? How do faculty and staff feel about the proposal? How will the work environment and the college's value system be affected? To ensure that the board explores all of these dimensions, the president, the chair, or another trustee could guide trustees through a process that intentionally analyzed and evaluated major policy questions through each frame. Over time the analysis of issues through multiple frames should become a standard yet explicit part of the way the board does business.

Ask One or More Trustees to Stand "Outside" and Monitor the Discussion. At first blush, this suggestion may seem at odds with the stress we have placed on inclusiveness. However, as long as the assignment rotates, we see no conflict. The outsider, or "critical evaluator," carefully listens to the discussion and charts the strengths and weaknesses of whatever proposals, permutations, and amendments are under consideration. The promises and pitfalls of each alternative could be charted by the monitor on newsprint, for example, so that everyone could literally see the pros and cons of each option. In this way, as the deliberations proceed, the board has a visual record of the discussion. Moreover, the process lessens the possibility that only the comments and concerns of the most vocal and forceful board members will be considered. Indeed, as a matter of board practice, the monitor should be encouraged to summarize the debate and to draw the board's attention to criticisms that were registered by a few yet ignored by the rest (a slight often experienced by women and members of minority groups).

Create "Safe" Internal Channels of Communication. Under certain circumstances, some boards might not even voice negative comments to record. The reluctance to probe the downside of a proposal or to express doubt can be attributed to several factors. Few trustees are eager to dampen the board's or the administration's enthusiasm for a proposal. No one wants to be branded a naysayer. And many trustees, sensitive to issues of status, are loath for personal or professional reasons to challenge a peer on the board.

One way to counteract these inhibitions would be to provide "safe" internal channels of communication, ways for trustees to convey concern with little or no risk of unease, intimidation, or rebuke. One approach, sometimes called the "nominal group" technique, invites board or committee members to provide anonymous, written responses to general or specific questions about the topic under consideration. The comments are then collected, read aloud, and discussed. Another approach, termed the "delphi" technique, involves iterative, brief, and often on-the-spot surveys where respondents are asked to rank-order preferences or alternative proposals. In each round the items with the least support are dropped until a consensus eventually emerges. Both methods enable trustees to raise questions and doubts in a relatively secure, low-risk fashion.

Designate a "Devil's Advocate" for Major Agenda Items. For a board more comfortable with open challenges, the president or the chairman of the board could publicly assign one or more trustees the role of devil's advocate whenever an important matter was under consideration. These trustees would be expected to identify flawed logic, erroneous assumptions, or other weaknesses in the arguments presented by trustees and staff. The devil's advocate would prod the board to identify any unanticipated changes in circumstances that might render the preferred course of action ill-advised. In short, what could go wrong? In the safety of that role, a trustee can be critical and skeptical with relative impunity. If the concerns expressed by the devil's advocate raised some hackles, the individual could later disavow those remarks rather easily and remind others that "I only did what I was asked to do."

Role Play. Once a board becomes acclimated to the idea of roles such as outside monitor and devil's advocate, the concept might be expanded to allow trustees to assume the perspectives of other key constituencies. For example, on a question like dormitory visitation or alcohol on campus, the board or a committee chair might ask a few trustees to adopt temporarily the roles of students, students' parents, and residence hall assistants. On a proposal to allocate a greater portion of salary increases based on merit, some trustees could "act" as senior professors, others as untenured faculty, and still others as department heads. In all cases, some board members would remain in the role of trustee to ask questions of these "visitors" and to evaluate responses from that perspective. Such exercises can be eye-openers that offer trustees a useful and often enjoyable way to diagnose a problem or evaluate a proposal from someone else's point of view.

Of course, to the extent that the board has regular interaction with these constituencies, role plays will be less necessary or useful. The next chapter describes a variety of ways for boards to communicate with students and faculty. For now, we would reiterate the recommendation offered earlier that, prior to any final decision on a significant issue, the board should systematically solicit and consider the views of those parties most likely to be affected by the decision and most likely to differ with the board's preferences.

Brainstorm. Most meetings of most boards are tightly scheduled, moderately regimented, and task-oriented. Trustees are preoccupied with the search for rational solutions to short-term problems or medium-range priorities. There is not much time or support for the board to "brainstorm," to think unbounded and unbridled about innovative, even radical and wild-eyed notions. Yet, the leaders of every organization need now and then to break loose from the constraints of current conditions, immediate concerns, and "reasonable" ideas. To borrow some phrases from Cohen and March (1974, p. 225) there needs to be time for "sensible foolishness" and "playfulness."

> Playfulness is the deliberate, temporary relaxation of rules in order to explore the possibilities of alternative rules. . . . In effect, we announce—in advance— our rejection of the usual objections to behavior that does not fit the standard model of intelligence. . . . A strict sense of purpose, consistency, and rationality limits our ability to find new purposes. Play relaxes that insistence to allow us to act "unintelligently" or "irrationally" or "foolishly" to explore alternative ideas of purposes and alternative concepts of behavioral consistency.

Very simply, brainstorming is a way to suspend for a period of time the normal rules of play. People are exhorted to generate fanciful and improbable ideas by the dozens. The process can entail a "silent brainstorm," where people anonymously submit ideas in advance, perhaps on index cards, to be collated and distributed as a springboard for further discussion. Or, the process can start with on-the-spot suggestions presented orally. In either case, criticisms are prohibited and judgments suspended, no matter how farfetched or half-baked the idea (Zander, 1982, p. 21). Once an exhaustive list has been developed, the group then tries to combine various possibilities and to wrestle exotic notions into the realm of reality. For instance, a college faced with an enrollment decline might brainstorm to envision not merely strategies to boost admissions, but drastically different futures for the institution. What if we moved or merged? Added or ended graduate programs? What if we closed, sold the campus, combined the proceeds with the endowment and reopened as a foundation dedicated to the college's mission and beliefs? How would we be different if we were dedicated to learning instead of schooling? Through such an exercise, old molds may be shattered, problems may be reconceptualized, the seeds of imaginative solutions may germinate, and the board may feel refreshed and reinvigorated to deal with the issues at hand.

Consult Outsiders. Despite their best efforts, the boards of independent colleges and other organizations where incumbents select most or all new members can become isolated and too like-minded. In fact, "the more cohesive the group and the more relevant the issue to the goals of the group, the greater is the inclination of the members to reject a nonconformist" (Janis,

1972, p. 3). Boards of trustees, therefore, as a general rule and especially on vital issues, may want to consult collectively or individually with outsiders who are well respected by the board but of a somewhat different stripe and perspective. The value of such consultation may be greatest when the stakes are highest, precisely when weak boards tend to pull inward and become most insular. Issues and analyses can be sharpened through presentations to the board by external experts or by trustees or presidents from other colleges that faced a similar problem and devised an unconventional solution. As long as no confidentialities are violated, the president or chair might recommend that each trustee discuss a particularly complex or nettlesome issue before the college with a trusted colleague not on the board and then report back on that person's reactions and suggestions.

DISCUSSION QUESTIONS AND EXERCISES

1. To be more analytical, sometimes it helps to think in terms of metaphors and analogies. Morgan (1986), for example, analyzed organizations as machines, organisms, brains, cultures, political systems, and psychic prisons. What metaphors come to mind to describe your institution and board? What do those metaphors suggest to you about the nature of the college and the role of the board? Thomas Gilmore, affiliated with the Wharton School of Business at the University of Pennsylvania, encourages organizational leaders to see relationships through analogies. For instance, BOARD is to PRESIDENT as GUIDE RAILS are to TRAINS or as FUEL is to ROCKETS. How would you complete that analogy? How about TRUSTEE is to BOARD as _____ is to _____, or BOARD is to INSTITUTION as _____ is to _____? At a retreat or a special segment of a board meeting devoted to self-study, trustees might openly compare analogies with one another to see whether any enjoy broad appeal. What are the characteristics and *assumptions* embedded in the most attractive analogies? What *behaviors* would one expect from a board that acted in accord with a particular analogy? What might be the *drawbacks* or *risks* associated with a board that behaved in this manner?

2. What would be your response if a newcomer to your board were to ask you "What are the unwritten rules for a trustee here? The unspoken things I really need to know to get along and be effective?" Looking collectively at your trustees' responses, what can you glean about the "frames" your board uses and how trustees "see" the board?

3. Think about how these frames affect the criteria and evidence the board would use to judge its own performance. For example, a rational frame may suggest that effectiveness be defined as attaining specified goals, whereas a political frame suggests satisfying dominant interest groups. How would your board define and assess "effective trusteeship"?

4. As a board, reexamine closely a situation in the last year or two where a complicated and crucial issue was before the board. How and where did the board pursue information? How did it go about analyzing the question? Determining the downside risks? Did some trustees or staff (erroneously) see an "obvious and correct" answer right away? What could the board have done differently and better?

5. What techniques does your board use to guard against "groupthink"? How could these procedures be strengthened?

5

The Political Dimension

DEFINITION

Competency 5 concerns a board's **political skills,** its ability to develop and maintain healthy relationships with key constituencies. In order to build such constructive relationships, effective boards: (1) respect the integrity of the governance process, (2) consult often and communicate directly with their key constituencies, and (3) attempt to minimize conflict and win-lose situations.

DESCRIPTION

The tranquil atmosphere and contemplative ambience of a college campus sometimes causes trustees (and academics) to forget that these institutions are complicated sociopolitical systems where various constituencies contend for power and influence. Board members should appreciate, however, that college presidents described their role as most like that of a mayor, a distinctly political position (Cohen and March, 1974, p. 62).

Colleges and universities *are* political systems. The academic organization is "a complex social structure that generates multiple pressures, there are many sources and forms of power and pressure that impinge on decision makers, there is a legislative stage that translates these pressures into policy, and there is a policy execution phase that generates feedback and potentially new conflicts" (Baldridge et al., 1978, p. 41). This model underscores a central feature of academic politics: numerous "publics" or constituencies with varied sources of legitimacy negotiate, compromise, and bargain until policies are established and implemented.

The process can often be intense. Indeed, a pundit once quipped that academic politics are often so bitter because the stakes are so small. Birnbaum (1988, p. 223) offered a more thoughtful explanation about academe's preoccupation with the political process:

> In most colleges and universities, the prevailing mood for most substantive matters is apathy—most people are not concerned about most issues most of the time. But one thing they are almost certain to be concerned about is process, because their right to participate and get involved is linked to their organizational status. The right way to do things is usually the way people *expect* it will be done. In higher education, process *is* substance, and administrators who forget that are likely to generate opposition to even the best ideas.

This admonition applies to trustees too. Indeed, we have the impression that when presidents or boards are confronted by votes of no confidence or otherwise vilified, the most heinous crimes in the eyes of the constituents are more often matters of process than substance.

Effective Boards Respect the Integrity of the Governance Process. Trustees of effective and midrange boards do not disregard the special qualities of academic politics or forget that "process is substance." When we asked board members to explain "What's most different about this college's decision-making process from other organizations with which you are equally familiar?" the trustees of effective and midrange boards articulated these critical differences.

> There's lots of meetings, no opportunity to decide things unilaterally, but that's the way things have to be in a university.

> My business decisions are made very quickly. It's a lot slower here. You have to listen and heed committees.

> We talk, talk, talk with others before we make decisions.

> What's most different? It's largely a matter of context. There is an awareness of responsibility toward a diverse constituency.

In other words, members of effective boards recognized that the decision-making process in academe moves more slowly and entails more discussion with more people from more constituencies when compared with other types of organizations.

Stronger boards also realized that trustee oversight of academic affairs, traditionally the faculty's province, required special sensitivity. Politically astute trustees on several boards recognized that the faculty had primary responsibility for academic affairs generally and the curriculum more specifically. "The board does not tell the college what to do with respect to the curriculum," commented one board member. "The faculty make their own decisions about curriculum issues," observed a trustee of another college.

In order to honor this principle, strong boards had to "swallow hard" on occasion and accept faculty recommendations that seemed questionable to the trustees. For example, one board reluctantly aproved a faculty recommendation to tenure a professor who, according to the president,

> raised hell in the papers and around the community, criticized the college and made scathing personal attacks on board members. Rather than reach into the process and get rid of him, which they certainly could have done, the board granted him tenure. They respected the value of faculty authority over personnel decisions.

A few trustees abstained—"that's as sticky as it ever gets," one said—but the others agreed that "the process had to be respected." The faculty on another campus proposed a controversial commencement speaker, someone characterized by the chairman of the board's campaign committee, as an "open advocate of the overthrow of America's economic system." Rather than summarily reject the nominee, the board asked the president to explain to the faculty committee the adverse consequences the invitation would have on community relations and the college's capacity to raise money. The board did not dispute the faculty's legitimate role in selecting a graduation speaker or the need for students to be exposed to a variety of views. The board asked only that the faculty be sensitive to the implications of the decision for the college and therefore recommend someone "a little less extreme." A speaker acceptable to the faculty and the board was eventually identified.

As illustrated by the incidents described here and by earlier vignettes such as the proposed abolition of required Bible courses and the appointment of a professor opposed to the college's fundamental tenets, effective boards did not "play dead" on academic matters. The preferred tactic to exercise oversight, however, was not to assert vigorously the board's "ultimate authority" over the faculty, the curriculum, and other academic domains. Instead, these boards provided guidance (and leadership) through inquiries, discussions, requests for information, and attempts to reach reasonable compromises—always within the larger framework of the institution's overall mission and always with explicit and authentic respect for "the process."

Interestingly, the practice of shared governance appears not only to be characteristic of institutions with effective boards but of "successful colleges" more generally. In a study of the relationship between institutional finances and organizational effectiveness, Anderson (1983, p.6) discovered that:

High levels of democratic governance were especially noticeable in the most effectively managed institutions and were generally absent in the least effective. . . . Professors must believe in their institutions; they must assume a sense of proprietorship for their campuses. Democratic governance may be the best means by which to cultivate this "ownership" attitude. . . . The level of institutional financial support and faculty salaries appear to have less effect on faculty morale than the meaningful participation of faculty in governance.

Institutions that aspire to be successful and to have effective boards might, therefore, emulate the shared governance model employed by colleges that have already reached these plateaus. Furthermore, an investment in democratic decision-making yields a handsome extra dividend: higher faculty morale. The process may not always be tidy or efficient, but the benefits seem to amply outweigh the costs.

Members of ineffective boards were less aware of the distinctive characteristics of academic politics. For instance, five of seven respondents from one weak board could not identify even one unique aspect of academic governance. Likewise, a trustee with more than thirty years' service on another incapable board replied, "I don't think the college's decision making process is so different. We have a strong president and administrative council now. They come to conclusions, hash it out among themselves, and by the time they present recommendations to the board it has been hashed out." In this case the chairman may well have been correct. If the process operates as described, there were not many differences from more hierarchical organizations. More significantly, though, that chairman appeared to be oblivious to the consequences of such patterns.

Further testimony to the greater political sensitivity of effective boards and some midrange boards was evidenced by the degree of the trustees' awareness of the board's many constituencies. Routinely, members of strong boards recited a rather comprehensive list of the board's numerous publics: "alumni, administrators, faculty, students, parents, and perhaps townsfolk in that order." Or, "the alumni, the administration, the faculty, the students, community leaders, and the board itself. The board represents all those who have a stake in the success of the college." Whatever the particular sequence, most respondents from most effective and midrange boards realized at a minimum that the board of trustees had many constituencies to serve and that these groups wanted to influence the board's decisions and the college's direction.

Trustees and presidents of ineffective boards were remarkably parochial on this score. In a few instances the list of key stakeholders never even extended beyond the board itself. Thus, some trustees identified the board's *only* major constituencies as "The president and the chairmen of the various board committees," "The executive committee of the board," and "The finance committee which is really the executive committee." One respondent, who cited "ourselves" as the board's "number one" constituency, also listed students, the administration, and the alumni, although the faculty was conspicuously omitted. Similarly, the faculty was ignored as a key constituency by five of eight members of an ineffectual board and by every respondent on one midrange board where several trustees also ignored all external constituencies such as alumni, donors, or townspeople. None of these trustee responses, however, epitomized myopia (and self-delusion) as starkly as the assertion by a president of a college with a weak board who claimed that no occasions had ever arisen where key constituencies had different views about matters of relevance to the board. "There are no such situations. None. Never."

Effective Boards Accept Responsibility for the Health of Relationships among Multiple Constituencies. Boards of trustees without much sensitivity to process and multiple constituencies were almost by definition unlikely to assume even partial responsibility for the need to develop smooth communication processes and healthy relationships among the college's major stakeholders. A trustee on an ineffective board could casually report, therefore, that when students and alumni opposed a "major decision we had made, we left it to the president to handle them. . . . We weren't concerned with students, who eventually graduate." In other words, the board was blithely indifferent toward the state of affairs between the college and students, since students are essentially transients. On another campus a member of an ineffective board reported a similar lack of interest in the faculty's welfare. "Sometimes a trustee will walk around the campus and talk to faculty members . . . but basically the board deals with the president, and he's responsible for taking care of faculty concerns." While a board might reasonably expect the president to be the pivotal link to the campus community, only members of ineffective boards seemed to be blind to the trustees' responsibility for strengthening constituency relationships.

In comparison, members of effective boards voiced a strong sense of duty that the board had to help develop and maintain constructive relationships among and between the college's various constituencies. The chairman of an exemplary board stated:

> You are being an effective board when you see a good administration and faculty team and they have good communication. . . . The board must feel responsible. The quality of relationships . . . [is] what we need to watch.

A trustee of another exceptionally able board expressed an even stronger opinion that trustees must understand and take into account the "legitimate concerns" of key constituencies since "the board *is responsible* to the president, the faculty, the students, the alumni, and the community." To translate these moral obligations into action, competent boards tried to maximize communication and consultation. As Henry Rosovsky, dean of the faculty of arts and sciences at Harvard, proclaimed in *The University: An Owner's Manual* (1990, p. 279), "Communication is a major form of accountability."

Effective Boards Consult Often and Communicate Directly with Key Constituencies. Effective and ineffective boards have distinctly different patterns of communication and consultation with institutional stakeholders. Effective boards routinely interacted and conferred with campus constituents, while ineffective boards did precisely the opposite.

Eager to relate directly to faculty and students, effective and midrange boards devised countless means to do so. Some of the mechanisms were ceremonial, such as an annual "faculty appreciation dinner." Others were informal and largely social, such as "an activity with students on Thursday nights" or "dinner in the homes of faculty members on Friday" at the college's expense. Usually, there were no set agendas or assigned topics at these gatherings and the primary purposes appeared to be quite simple, namely, to become better acquainted and to discuss topics of mutual interest, like general education, a global economy, or the role of sororities and fraternities on ethnically and racially diverse campuses. Faculty and students seemed to understand that these were not occasions to bleat, complain, or gossip. No president or trustee we interviewed reported any abuses and many cited advantages, such as "the opportunity for wealthy trustees to visit professors' homes and see personally how faculty live on $35,000 a year."

In addition to casual, social activities, many effective and midrange boards also had more formal structures for trustees to communicate directly with faculty and students. Students and faculty members frequently served as participants or observers on board committees, and campus leaders normally attended all board meetings. Why did the more competent boards establish such arrangements? Among the reasons provided by trustees of effective boards were:

Relations with the faculty are improving but still have a long way to go. Very few faculty know much about the board and vice-versa . The board decided that we need more contact with faculty.

We wanted students to have tremendous exposure to the college's decision-making process.

There is a definite move now to get closer to faculty through meetings and forums and to hear directly from them, not just through the administration.

We're trying harder now to overcome past problems by meeting more often with faculty, both one-on-one and on panels dealing with controversial topics.

In one unusual case, the board held an executive session with officers of the faculty senate, without the president, each time the board met, although the chairman noted that "I do not approve of that arrangement."

Besides these efforts to involve students and faculty in the board's regularly scheduled discussions, stronger boards usually included constituent representatives at special events such as board retreats to develop long-range plans, to set priorities for a capital campaign, or to reexamine the college's mission. Indeed, one board held a retreat, regarded as "a big success," that was devoted solely to faculty-trustee relations. Other boards convened collegewide forums on occasion to discuss particularly important and pervasive issues. The presence of faculty, students, and alumni at such retreats and forums was as natural to competent boards as the idea was alien to ineffective boards. Broad participation by diverse constituencies was regarded by effective boards as essential to an enlightened discussion and a smooth process. Illustrative of that point of view, the past chairman of an excellent board stated:

> We try to sustain good channels of communication with all these groups through inviting them to participate on our committees, both standing committees and ad hoc work groups that address specific issues. A good example would be our current task force on communications and computers, which includes students, faculty, representatives from the college's principal computer vender, and some trustees. Another example would be our meetings with the city council to discuss economic and social impacts of the college on the community.

At the earliest signs that debate on a particular topic might evolve into a dispute or a crisis, effective boards were especially certain to broaden the channels of communication and to enlarge the circle of consultation. Irrespective of the specific nature of the controversy, competent boards responded similarly. On one campus the issue was divestment.

> Not all trustees and alumni felt the same way. There was even a bit of disagreement within the faculty and student bodies. So we opened up lines of communication, established a faculty-student-trustee committee and came up with recommendations most of us could support.

On another campus the issue (described in chapter 1) concerned the president's decision to withdraw an appointment offered to a professor who was personally unable to support the college's denominational mission and who was openly committed to changing it. As recounted by a trustee officer,

> The board decided that we had to resolve matter before it got totally out of hand, so it agreed with the chairman's suggestion that we call a series of open town meetings with the college constituencies. Our objective was to get out of the win-lose stance and in some way that we could come together. There were

several open discussions with faculty, students, trustees, staff, and alumni present. People were able to share their concerns freely and hear others. . . . That process led to a new sense of our mission and its influence on the college, as well as a much better atmosphere of communication and trust among all the members of our college family. We have seen evidence of that in our subsequent interaction.

With the consent and encouragement of the president, effective boards *initiated* communications with significant stakeholders on and off campus. Effective boards wanted to understand and incorporate the viewpoints of other constituencies into the trustees' deliberations. Moreover, adept trustees were persuaded that when the various parties collaborated on a common concern, the level of trust usually increased. In a comment representative of one board's sentiment, the chairman remarked, "We seek the faculty's opinion because we respect them, and I believe that they are aware of that respect."

If effective boards inclined toward an inclusive philosophy of "the more the merrier," ineffective and some midrange boards tended to withdraw and to assume that "the fewer the better." Most trustees on weaker (and some midrange) boards were extremely reluctant to have direct communication with various constituencies, especially students and faculty. Their reasons varied. In many instances, trustees worried that open dialogue with members of the campus community would undercut the president and violate the precept, typical of "the majority of private colleges" (Wood, 1985, p. 101), that the institution should be run like a corporation. Trustees partial to that model believed that "the board should relate to the president. " (p.109). Thus, the chairman of the academic affairs committee of one mediocre board contended that faculty

> should be *appropriately* involved in development of policy and that appropriateness stops at the board room door. They make their contributions through the college's decision making process but not through direct formal contact with the board.

A trustee on another board offered a similar remark about students. "I don't talk directly with students. I rely on the administration to tell me what students think." In other words, faculty and student opinions were to be heard by the board only through intermediaries and never first-hand.

Several weak boards acceded to the president's desire to be the sole conduit to faculty and students. Some presidents worried that face-to-face conversations between the board and faculty or students would open a floodgate of direct communications and thus undermine the presidency, confound the issue at hand, and confuse unsophisticated trustees. Thus, one president introduced the board to a faculty document on the college's mission without any professors present and then relayed the board's reaction to the faculty without any trustees present. Only a few trustees on ineffective boards complained about such arrangements. For example, one trustee regretted that "the board has to depend too much on what the president tells us. The president seems to be nervous about direct contact between the board and the faculty. It might cause mischief, but it might be worth the risk." A member of another weak board, where the president controlled and limited the channels of communication, expressed a similar opinion. "For some reason, the president seems to want to constrain the board's exchange with faculty and not let it open up very much. I don't understand why he's taking that stance." In the main, though, ineffective boards did not attempt to alter the president's determination to be the trustees' go-between vis-a-vis campus constituencies. More often, those trustees merely lamented that "the faculty sees the board as remote and out of touch with their concerns," but that was because "the faculty doesn't understand our role and doesn't seem to appreciate our efforts to communicate with them."

A third reason that some boards had little or no contact with members of the campus community was that a few immoderate trustees disdained student and faculty opinion whether offered directly or indirectly. With only a thinly veiled contempt for dialogue with these constituencies, the chairman of an ineffective board declared, "I tell faculty and students, 'My perspective is the next hundred years, yours is the next four years. Thank you for your views, but my concern is not your time frame.' " So much for mutual respect and campus morale.

Effective Boards Attempt to Minimize Conflict and Avoid Win-Lose Situations. Communication and consultation with essential stakeholders serves dual purposes: to improve the quality of information and discussion and to smooth the political process. In order to achieve the latter objective, effective boards adopted two other important behavioral norms: when necessary, proceed slowly so that a consensus may form and, whenever possible, avoid actions and decisions that threaten to divide the board or the campus into winners and losers. As the chairman of an effective board enunciated this principle, "We try to be careful to avoid partisanship or factions, situations that come to be defined as pitting one group against another."

A popular maxim about the for-profit sector holds that most American executives devote about 20 percent of their energies to matters of process and the rest to problems of implementation, while in Japan the ratio is exactly the reverse, which may help explain why Japanese corporations experience fewer problems of implementation and greater productivity.[1] In any case, the attitudes and behaviors of effective trustees we interviewed more closely resembled the Japanese approach to reaching decisions.

---

[1] Attitudes may be changing. Kanter (1983, p. 231) reports that the "enterprising" American manager, recognizing the need to attend to process, "may now be spending as much time in meetings, both formal and individual, as he or she did to get a project launched."

There was a marked tendency on the part of strong boards not to rush to closure or to foreclose options on crucial policy questions. For instance, one effective board worked long and hard with the faculty on revising criteria for promotion and tenure. There were, recalled a former board chairman,

> conflicts among the faculty on these issues, so we had to proceed cautiously and resist those who pressed for quick decisions. We took a year on some of the more sensitive problems, and on most we came to a mutually agreeable conclusion.

On one issue, however, the faculty could not reach resolution as a minority insisted that assistant professors should be eligible for tenure:

> We tried everything we could to avoid bringing it to a vote in order to avoid hard feelings, but it became apparent that that issue was not going to be resolved mutually. . . . So the obvious answer of coming to a quick vote had to be postponed in order to work out mutually acceptable solutions wherever possible and avoid as much as possible having people see themselves as winners or losers. By the time we finally came to a vote on that single remaining problem, I think that almost everyone was relieved to have it over with.

Another effective board followed a similar tack on curriculum reform. "We didn't force the issue, like you can in business," declared the chairman of the board. Instead, "we set up a process to explore the curriculum" that enabled faculty, trustees, and the president to "work on these issues together." After nearly a year had elapsed, the faculty still wanted to "rework the recommendations a little more." Disappointed by the delay, yet patient, the chairman emphasized that, while the process was painfully slow, "eventually we'll have something that we can all buy."

Effective boards basically attempted to *minimize* rather than *overcome* resistance. "Most of the time," the chairman of an effective board commented, "we can find some way to work out compromises so that the basic concerns of our constituencies can be met and harmonized with the mission of the college." Stronger boards appeared to be more attuned to Kotter and Schlesinger's (1979) advice that people who want to lessen resistance to change should move slowly, particularly under circumstances where: (1) there could be considerable opposition from powerful resistors; (2) where the initiators of change needed information and commitment from others; and (3) where the stakes were comparatively low and did not jeopardize organizational survival. In those situations, the authors argue, leaders should move deliberately, engage others, and allow a mutually acceptable plan to emerge. By and large, these conditions characterized most of the problematic situations described by trustees we interviewed. That is, faculty or students (and occasionally alumni or townspeople) could have mustered considerable resistance, the faculty's expertise and the campus community's cooperation were often essential to success, and none of the issues posed a crisis of such magnitude that the board had to act immediately to save the school. Thus, the boards' change strategies were well-suited to the circumstances.

Ineffective boards seemed far less concerned about the need to generate a consensus, to compromise, or to avert a showdown. Often, weaker boards apparently *assumed* that the most appropriate (and maybe the only) response to differences of opinion was to call for a vote, count the ballots, and declare a winner. Here are only a few examples of that mindset.

> We disagreed on the choice of a president and on whether to explore joining the state system. When that happens, we take a vote, and the majority *rules*.

> When students wanted to be allowed to drink on this campus, the board was very divided. We voted and the majority *won*. But the discussion didn't change anyone's mind.

> This used to be a two-city board with the people in one city as the power brokers. The trustees from the other city who did the work got fed up with that. We don't meet in the second city any more. If they want to participate, *they have to come to us*.

As the italicized words indicate, there were winners and losers with little regard for the process or the fallout which included bruised egos, hardened factions, and low commitment to the adopted policy or plan.

As a way to conclude this discussion and to accentuate the disparity between the political competencies of effective and ineffective boards, we juxtapose two critical incidents. Each concerned a campus controversy and, importantly, both were offered in response to the same question: "Can you describe an incident where the board was particularly effective in handling an important situation?" The first report quotes the former chairman of a weak board, the second quotes the chairman of the finance committee of an exemplary board. (Portions of the text are italicized to highlight the dissimilarities.)

> There was a really bad period of disruption on the campus. The students *took over* the campus newspaper and printed all kinds of destructive stuff. They *demanded* shared governance and actually came right in here and tried to *take over* our board meeting. The faculty was right with them. The faculty formed a union and made all kinds of demands. There were many long and painful discussions. Some of the trustees got so angry or upset that *they resigned. A few of us had the courage to stick it out and hold the line. We refused to let them take us over.* We called a private meeting with the president. He was siding with the faculty and was just making things worse, *so we let him go. One of our guys* got in touch with a former president, and he filled in while we looked for someone to *take over.* We found a strong disciplinarian, someone

who could *reassert control and stability* and get this place back on its feet. Our little "steering committee" led this process. . . . The courage of a few board members was the key to it all.

Laced with the rhetoric of confrontation and cliques, this account epitomizes Argyris's (1976, pp. 18–19) concept of "Model I behavior" where the goals are to assert control, maximize victories and minimize defeats, and achieve self-determined purposes. Argyris concluded that these behaviors ultimately lead to increased defensiveness and decreased effectiveness and, indeed, this college has terminated yet another president, endured unabated faculty strife, and incurred the sanction of a national professional association. Insofar as a board's actions express institutional values, one has to wonder about the message students, faculty, and staff are to glean when the board of a church-related college obsesses about control and where, if all else fails, trustees resign, dismiss the president, or both.

In the second incident, the campus controversy was about divestment.

There was no ugliness, but the students were pressing the college to divest. For example, students formed a circle and held hands around the site where the board meets. The Investment Committee told the board that they were being pushed and wanted to meet with students. We felt *we wanted students to understand our position and we wanted to understand theirs*. We thought the best way to do that was to meet with the students. . . . *The whole committee was involved because we thought it was healthy to have an open meeting. We did not want to let the issue simmer*. It was far better to have an open discussion. The meeting took place in the snack bar where there is also a fireplace. We sat in a semicircle. *The Investment Committee chairman and a student presided together*. There were about thirty-five or forty students and we met for two or three hours. It was quite informal. No one was on the defensive. . . . We always have an open door with students. *Most of all we want to establish a better rapport with students and we wanted them to have a better understanding of the issue*. We didn't have an incident, we had instead an understanding of the issues. . . . *Our attitudes are not set in concrete*. We try hard to be flexible. *We want to know why students believe what they do*.

Here was an accessible, attentive board, eager to converse rather than confront, a board disposed to empower rather than control. The contrast with the other incident could not be more extreme.

Incidentally, some presidents and trustees might be wary of an open forum between board members and students where the CEO does not preside (or even attend). Yet, this president had only praise for the board. "They were effective because board members genuinely educated themselves and moved into a position of leadership. They were willing to venture into an open setting and not hide behind the administration. . . . They were a serious, sincere, dedicated set of people with an obvious concern, *willing to make themselves vulnerable to students.*"

SUGGESTIONS

Philosophically at least, most people readily accept concepts like openness, trust, and involvement as vital to an enlightened political process. Everyone wants to do "the right thing." More often, problems arise when "extraordinary circumstances" require that these principles be temporarily suspended or when, under the guise of communication and consultation, the actual goals are manipulation, cooptation, or token participation. In a word, authenticity counts. As Fisher and Brown (1988, p. 64) stated, "The simplest and most powerful rule of thumb is to consult the relationship partner. Really consult. Ask advice before making a decision—and listen carefully."

As a very first step toward an authentic process, all parties need to be clear about mutual expectations and about the context and objectives of their interaction. The board should make certain, therefore, that trustees are oriented (and periodically reoriented) to the peculiar characteristics of academic decision making. As we recommended in chapter 1, trustee orientation programs should include presentations by faculty and student leaders about the precepts of shared governance so that trustees understand the stakeholders' perspectives. In turn, the board should make plain the purposes of constituent participation as specific situations arise. Is it to seek opinions, counsel, consensus, or approval? The question then becomes "*How* do we seek input most effectively?"

Channels of Communication. We delineated above several techniques, such as joint task forces and attendance at board retreats, that are used by effective boards to communicate and consult with key stakeholders. In addition, we have gathered other noteworthy approaches from campuses we visited as researchers or consultants and from conversations we have had with board members at conferences and workshops. These specific tactics will be described shortly. First, though, we would like to offer a general observation.

Trustees on one hand and faculty, students, and most staff on the other are normally more or less strangers to one another. At a distance, stereotypes and misperceptions develop rather easily. Thus, more than a few trustees we encountered viewed faculty as underworked, eccentric eggheads disconnected from the "real world," and students were regarded as impulsive, transient, idealistic, and naive. Conversely, many students and faculty perceived trustees to be extraordinarily affluent captives of the administration, detached guardians of the status quo, motivated to serve by some ill-defined and protective self-interest. In reality, none of these images withstands close scrutiny. Yet without the opportunity to meet, talk, or collaborate, stereotypes will persist and all of the campus constituencies will badly underestimate one another's dedication and commitment to the institution's well-being. If for no other reason then, boards of trustees should consider several options to communicate and consult with constituencies.

1. DISTRIBUTE ANNUALLY A PROFILE OF BOARD MEMBERS. The profile which could be part of an in-house publication, the student newspaper, an alumni magazine, or all three, should provide a brief biographical sketch of each trustee, with some statement about why the individual decided to serve on the board. A little information about trustees' interests, background, and family helps to humanize the board and to identify potential topics of conversation in the event that one should one ever be face-to-face with a trustee.

2. DISTRIBUTE AN ANNUAL BOARD REPORT AND AN ANNUAL BOARD AGENDA. Not many members of the campus or larger community know much about what a board has done or plans to do. A report by the chairman of the board or the executive committee will help constituents to understand the board's and president's accomplishments, disappointments, and intentions. Aware of the board's priorities, some faculty and students may even submit useful suggestions and creative ideas. For the same reasons, the college should disseminate (with the exception of confidential matters) the agenda and minutes from board meetings.

These suggestions enable the board to communicate with the institution's stakeholders. In order to complete the loop, the board might also:

3. PERMIT STUDENTS AND FACULTY TO SERVE ON BOARD COMMITTEES. A 1988 survey by the Association of Governing Boards revealed that the percentage of independent colleges with student and faculty members was as follows:

BOARD COMMITTEE	% FACULTY	%STUDENTS
Executive	5	3
Academic Affairs	47	25
Student Affairs	35	47
Finance	17	11

The data did not reveal whether or not faculty and students had the right to vote. Inasmuch as committees typically recommend to the board, often based on guidance from senior staff, we see little danger and considerable political gain if student and faculty committee members were allowed to vote.

We do not, however, advocate that local students or faculty serve as board members, as slightly more than 1 percent of the boards of independent colleges now permit (AGB, 1985, pp. 20–21). That arrangement does invite conflict of interest on matters such as salaries, tuition levels, or graduation requirements. Why court the risk when there are numerous other safer means to gain the benefits of faculty and student participation? On the other hand, we commend the appointment to the board of recent graduates or professors from comparable institutions.

4. *INVITE FACULTY, STUDENT, AND ALUMNI LEADERS PERIODICALLY TO ADDRESS THE BOARD.* Just as the board might issue an annual report on priorities and progress, officers of the student government, faculty senate, and alumni council might be invited to do likewise orally before the board. Occasionally the board may wish to learn firsthand the views of constituencies likely to be most immediately affected by a decision under consideration by the board. On crucial or controversial issues, the board should insist that the president explain both the process of consultation and the dominant sentiments of all concerned parties. Remember too that a board that denies students and faculty an opportunity to speak may, as was the case with some ineffective boards, be confronted with a demand, demonstration, or sit-in to do so. In that regard, Alexander (1986, p. 472) offers a provocative suggestion: "Formal and explicit advisory powers should be assigned to student bodies and faculty senates, according to which a vote by a certain percentage would require that an issue be discussed and eventually voted upon by the university governing board."

5. *EXPLORE A "NATURAL HABITAT."* In addition to various receptions or dinners, trustees may wish to visit the natural environs of students and professors: dormitories, classrooms, and laboratories. Thus, one college asks each board member to "adopt a dorm," which means that the trustee spends a couple of hours in a residence hall with students, just prior to board meetings, to discuss whatever topics the students or trustees may wish to raise. The same idea could be applied to departments or schools. In addition, with the faculty member's consent, the president or provost could arrange for trustees to attend classes or seminars occasionally to see how education—the college's main business—actually takes place. We believe that most faculty would be delighted to invite a trustee to class and that most trustees will find the experience instructive. (As a matter of courtesy to both faculty and students, visitations should always be by invitation.) Trustees might also reverse the process from time to time and invite campus leaders to visit their work sites to discuss topics of import to members of their organizations. In that way, students and teachers may have a better appreciation for the trustees' indigenous environment and culture.

While these various avenues of communication promise to be beneficial to all the constituencies involved, we stipulate that the interaction cannot be left wholly unstructured. Trustees should not be turned loose to collar and confer with faculty and students. Nor, however, should all discussions be "regulated" by the administration, as show-and-tell sessions tend to be. The board and the president need to strike a balance. For *informal* exchanges, the president should arrange some events where casual conversations about topics of mutual interest are the natural order of the day. These are the times for trustees to discover common interests with students and faculty or to exchange views on topics as varied as the impact of technology on instruction, the effect of tuition increases on student diversity, or current world events. For *formal* exchanges on matters related to specific institutional policies and plans, the college under the president's leadership should utilize established structures (e.g., students and faculty on board committees, open forums) that permit regular commerce between the board and campus constituencies. In consultation with the board and senior staff, the president may determine the process and the agenda, but the CEO should not screen the participants or control the content. These institutionalized channels of communication should also serve well when provocative issues arise, although at times of genuine crisis ad hoc mechanisms may be needed as well.

In all cases, boards would be wise to observe one basic guideline: The president should be instrumental in developing, maintaining, and refining the processes that enable trustees to communicate and consult directly with stakeholders. As an insightful trustee of an otherwise ineffective board lamented about the president's penchant to isolate the board from campus constituencies, "We have not become sufficiently linked with the community, with students and faculty, to know the college." How does a board that, by its own admission, does not "know the college" govern the institution? Not effectively, we would answer. Boards must be certain to develop and sustain numerous two-way avenues of communication with key stakeholders.

6. MONITOR THE HEALTH OF RELATIONSHIPS. Sophisticated boards monitor a variety of institutional performance indicators such as financial ratios, admissions yield, graduation rates, and tenure levels, to name a few.[2] These are hard data and incontestable facts and therefore may appeal to trustees comfortable with quantifiable information and "the bottom line."

There are, however, some softer concepts, like the quality of relationships, that are at least as important. Some can be very loosely translated into quantitative data. Crude proxies for the state of a college's relations with crucial constituencies might include: admissions yield for prospective students, transfer, attrition, and graduation rates for current students, voluntary turnover rates for faculty and staff, and participation rates in the annual fund for alumni.

---

[2] *Strategic Decision Making: Key Questions and Indicators for Trustees* (Association of Governing Boards, 1987) provides an excellent guide on data boards should monitor.

On the matter of faculty morale, the Educational Testing Service developed and refined an "institutional functioning inventory" that has a specific scale to measure morale. Rice and Austin (1988) used a different instrument, a "job satisfaction index," to measure faculty satisfaction and morale at 140 liberal arts colleges.

Among the colleges in the Austin/Rice sample, several coincidentally overlapped with the present study. Of the three institutions we visited that had low morale and low satisfaction in the Austin/Rice survey, two had ineffective boards and the other had a midrange board. (At a fourth college with a very weak board, the college agreed to participate in the study but no faculty even bothered to respond.) Of the four institutions that had a relatively positive faculty attitude, two had effective boards and two were midrange. By no means do we wish to suggest a causal or absolute relationship between effective boards and high faculty morale. Nevertheless, there does appear to be a discernible, though hardly perfect, pattern of association.

We provide these observations in order to make the larger point that boards of trustees should encourage and, if need be, nudge the administration to periodically assess and report to the board the state of the college's relationships with important stakeholders. By the same token, the board should consider whether or not to seek information intermittently about stakeholders' perceptions of the board. Techniques could range from casual conversations with constituency leaders to focus groups conducted by a third-party to opinion surveys. Rather than seek an appraisal of the board's overall performance per se, the paramount goal of such efforts should be to gather feedback about the perceived appropriateness of the board's priorities and the perceived effectiveness of the board's communication with constituencies. In the process, the board should learn a good deal about what works best, and the very act of soliciting the opinions of others should help improve constituent relations.

DISCUSSION QUESTIONS AND EXERCISES

1. Ask each trustee to write down a few phrases that best characterize the board's "operating style." Compare the answers to see whether there is a general consensus about how the board does business, and then discuss how (if at all) the board's mode of operation differs from businesses and other organizations familiar to members of the board.

2. Who are the board's key internal and external constituencies? What are the legitimate claims of each on the governance process? That is, in what areas or domains should they reasonably expect to have a voice in decision making?

3. How often and by what means does the board communicate with these constituencies? How effective are these forms of communication from the point of view of: (1) the board, (2) the president, (3) the stakeholders? How would you respond if a responsible student or professor asked, "Are you interested in my thinking on this issue and, if so, how should I communicate it to you?"

4. Think of situations that involved the board where at least two key constituencies (or two groups within the same constituency) had strongly held but different views on an important matter. Try to describe in detail what the board did in that situation? Whom did it consult? What role did it play? Was the board able to effect a compromise, or were there winners and losers?

5. What do you think the average faculty member on your campus would say about the quality of board-faculty relations? How accurate do you think that opinion is? What do you think the board has done to lead faculty to this particular assessment? Would the faculty leadership respond much differently? Ask the same questions about other constituencies such as students and alumni.

6

The Strategic Dimension

DEFINITION

The final competency of effective trusteeship concerns the **strategic dimension,** a board's ability to envision and shape institutional direction. To play that role effectively, competent boards cultivate and concentrate on processes that sharpen institutional priorities and ensure a strategic approach to the organization's future. As a result, these boards focus on matters of significant magnitude and anticipate potential problems before the issues become urgent.

DESCRIPTION

As recently as twenty years ago, management was a new and largely unwelcome concept on college campuses. Many, if not most, faculty and academic administrators believed that increased efforts to apply the tools and techniques of business to higher education would be misguided, inappropriate, and a threat to the traditions of collegiality and shared governance. Today, however, most college administrators and trustees comfortably invoke the language of management science: marketing, cost control, productivity, and above all else, strategic planning. Indeed, strategy has become such a commonplace concept in the not-for-profit sector that the word—like excellence, quality, and distinctiveness—has taken on too many connotations to be useful without a specific definition. Thus, before we describe the strategic dimension, we need to define what we mean by "strategy."

We favor one of the earliest definitions, offered in 1971 by Kenneth Andrews, then a professor at the Harvard Business School (pp.18–19).

> Corporate strategy is the pattern of decisions in a company that determines and reveals its objectives, purposes, or goals, produces the principal policies and plans for achieving those goals, and defines the range of business the company is to pursue . . . preferably in a way that focuses resources to convert distinctive competence into competitive advantage.

Twelve years later in a landmark book titled *Academic Strategy*, Keller (1983, p. 75) adopted a similar perspective. "Strategy means agreeing on some aims and having a plan . . . to arrive at a destination through the effective use of resources. . . . [It is] understanding what business you are in, or want to be in, and deciding what is central for the health, growth, and quality of the organization." To realize a strategy requires that leaders manage attention and create focus for all of an organization's participants. (Bennis and Nanus, 1985). By these definitions, the activities of able boards were very strategic.

Effective Boards Attend to Strategy. Nearly every treatise on trusteeship advises that the board's time and attention are scarce resources that should be allocated to a few core issues "which really make a difference between success and failure" (AGB, 1987, p. 3). Moreover, since most independent colleges face a rather dynamic social, political, and economic environment, one might assume that boards necessarily, even instinctively, concentrate on a few truly crucial, strategic questions generated by the president and the board's leaders. Sadly, that was not the case among many boards.

When asked to list the board's priorities for the next three to five years, more than a few trustees of weak and midrange boards admitted with remarkable candor that their board's priorities were trivial or unknown. Board agendas were crowded with routine matters of relatively little significance, such as minor renovations to the physical plant, approval of easements, or the reconfiguration of courses for a particular academic minor. While these unrelated and comparatively unimportant items created an aura of activity, there was little sense of purpose and priority. A member of one midrange board supposed that the president had some paramount goals, though "none have been really articulated. I'm sure there were some three years ago, but I don't know what they were. . . . There must have been some kind of capital campaign." Elsewhere, a trustee with eleven years' service commented, "I'm not sure that any priorities have been expressed," a perception echoed by the president.

> Priorities have not been identified. Historically, the board has focused on fiduciary responsibilities. . . . To give you an example of where they are, they spent most of my first meeting here talking about the senior picture book and

why it came out so late last year. They have sort of thought of themselves as the college's grandparents. The administration are the parents and the students are the children.

On financially fragile campuses, members of ineffective boards often cited "survival of the college" or "growth" as the board's sole priority. Although a reasonable goal for economically tenuous entities, survival should not be confused with direction any more than a corporation's sales target should be construed as its strategy. While several members of one ineffective board stated that "the budget determines priorities," a more strategic perspective might assert that priorities determine the budget.

Whereas ineffective boards were uncertain about organizational priorities, stronger boards ensured that there was a process in place to identify and pursue crucial issues. Although the details of the process differed from college to college, there were some common features. Each was designed to be *focused, inclusive, and comprehensive*, and the priorities that emerged were *interrelated, central, and strategic*.

Whether the process was initiated by the president, the chair of the board, or a trustee committee, effective boards followed a broadly similar course that started with the institution's mission. As a trustee of one college declared, "The board has one priority: to preserve the college's clarity of purpose. There is no board agenda apart from this. This has always been our priority and always will be." Thus, the members of one effective board were able to debate "the particulars of the college's plan within the context of our overall determination to be the best liberal arts college in the region. This priority has not changed." In other words, the board did not lose sight of its target: mission and strategy.

Moreover, the campus community took collective aim. Trustees and presidents from almost all of the most effective boards emphasized that the board and other key stakeholders played integral and collaborative roles in the development of strategy. One board chairman described a typical process that occurred over a three-year period and culminated with the adoption by the board of a five-year plan:

> The then board chair was the one who first suggested that we develop a plan, and the president put the structure together. We had a planning meeting off campus which was attended by trustees, administrators, faculty, students, and alumni, and a facilitator. We spent a day talking about the college's strengths and weaknesses and about what changes we'd like to make. . . . The issues we dealt with are important to the college, and we feel as trustees that what we do is important.

A college president associated with another effective board detailed with equal enthusiasm a very similar process.

> We began a thorough process of strategic planning about two years ago. . . .
> We've involved each of the constituencies of the college and gone over the
> needs and concerns of every part of the system. We have spelled out some goals
> and objectives, along with specifying the resources we need in the future in
> order to make them possible . . . This has been a more comprehensive and
> thorough process than we've ever done before, so everyone feels quite involved
> and committed to the conclusions.

On still another campus, the board and the president together designed a
process that engaged faculty, staff, and trustees in an all-day retreat to
clarify the college's strategic priorities for a capital campaign.

In each of these instances, the process was inclusive and the board was
active. Rather than address questions of strategy only at arm's length, effective boards played an instrumental role in launching and supporting a con-
sultative planning process and in developing strategic initiatives. They par-
ticipated actively in collaborative discussions about topics such as mission
statements, the specificity of goals and objectives, means to monitor the
internal and external environment, and problems likely to affect the college
in the 1990s. From these discussions, the trustees and the campus community generated ideas and forged an overall corporate strategy—a *pattern* of
decisions that revealed and advanced organizational priorities.

Thus, effective boards allocated their attention purposefully and analyzed issues with a keen awareness of the relationship between the matter at
hand and larger questions of corporate strategy. The perspective of stronger
boards was comprehensive and holistic, whereas weaker boards were disposed to tackle issues in a disconnected, and sometimes almost random,
fashion. This difference can best be illustrated by one board, now very
effective, whose approach shifted over time from linear to strategic. The
current chairman, a senior trustee, and the president all depicted similar
changes in the board's behavior.

> In past years, we went at our concerns in a different way. We worked on
> individual, separate issues. If a building needed renovation, we raised the
> money to do it. But now we try to deal with things as part of a total plan, a
> coordinated program for the future of the college. The needs of that same
> building would be looked at now in terms of its place as one issue among
> many, and its needs weighed together along with numerous other emerging
> needs and the flow of resources.

> There were times in the past when we tended to see things in terms of survival,
> which led us to try some things that we really weren't in a position to do well.
> Those days are over now, and the commitment to quality in everything is clear.
> We have a good process of examining the various needs and recommendations
> that come up and evaluating them in the context of our total plan for the
> college.

In the past, we tended to address our needs one at a time, in sequence, rather than seeing them as interrelated parts of a total system requiring a comprehensive plan and concurrent consideration. So whatever the specific items on the agenda three years ago, they were isolated decisions. Now the difference is that we try to look at things in the context of our total plan for the college.

However absorbed by such questions of strategy, effective boards did not allow themselves to become ensnared in the thickets of operational details. To the contrary, by focusing on the entire forest, effective boards rarely tampered with the individual trees. To paraphrase one member of a strong board, "We have to be aware of the total system, how one thing affects another, but we should not get our hands into the day-to-day activities of the college." And since effective boards concentrated on the long-term, there was hardly any inclination to meddle with the short-term.

The behaviors of effective boards differed considerably from some experts' advice about the board's proper role in crafting an academic strategy. Rosovsky's three-hundred-page *Owner's Manual* (1990) for a university, as an example, mentions boards of trustees only in the preface and later in a footnote. Grouped with alumni and donors, boards are described summarily as the body "that formally ratif(ies) major policies (p. 14)." As to whether the board should be involved in strategy formulation, Keller (1983, p. 150) contended:

It depends on the activism of the trustees. Several campuses I visited have included one or two board members in key strategy sessions. The governing board obviously has a role to play in major policy decisions. But because board members are usually busy executives themselves, they often prefer to make more rapid yes-no decisions and let their chief executive work out the slow, careful deliberations.

Whatever conventional wisdom may hold, the effective boards we visited wanted and indeed insisted upon a level of participation that extended well beyond "rapid yes-no decisions." Sensitive to academic protocol and reluctant to become enmeshed in administrative details, the attention of stronger boards was riveted on matters of overall corporate strategy.

In fact, the boards that merely ratified major policy recommendations with "rapid yes-no decisions" or ignored strategy altogether were largely ineffective, tended to be dominated by the president, and often voiced exasperation over the lack of trustee involvement. Typical of ineffectual boards, one trustee remarked that "our board reviews, critiques, and votes on the president's ideas, but we do not initiate or originate plans. This is about the way this board has always operated." An even more passive role was sketched by the chairman and president of an extremely weak board. "The board doesn't declare priorities. I do," proclaimed the chairman. Interestingly, the president had a similar view of the board, but a strikingly different perception of the source of institutional priorities. "How are priorities determined? Through me and my associates. I oversee everything for the board. I frame it for them. When they're good, I leave them alone." With such unilateral and incompatible perspectives, perhaps the subsequent resignation of both the president and the chairman was not entirely coincidental. Moreover, the board then reversed direction on a dramatic and strategic action the now-departed "leaders" had initiated.

While many members of ineffective boards seemed resigned to inactive and even submissive roles, a few openly expressed frustration over the board's inability to rise above "remediation and emergencies" in order to do "more planning for the future." Others lamented the "absence of orderly progress or sustained and careful attention" to strategic questions or the board's penchant to "waste time on unimportant matters." As a consequence of these behaviors, one trustee ruefully acknowledged, "I can't think of an instance when the board as a whole took action that made a significant, positive difference." Quite a self-indictment.

Effective Boards Anticipate Problems and Act Before Issues Become Urgent. As a trustee of an exemplary board remarked, "You have to be aware of issues and trends as they are emerging and sense where things are headed." While no trustee or president can foresee the future, effective boards appreciated the need to seek data and clues and to pose questions about the months and years ahead that would enable the institution to anticipate problems and opportunities and to then act seasonably. In other words, boards contributed strategic leadership through *information, insight, and inquiry.*

Consistent with the notion that a strategic perspective emphasizes the relationship of "whole organization to whole environment" (Cope, 1987, p. 3), several strong boards focused on the institution's external world. For instance, as reported by the past chairman of one college's board, the trustees and president

> began a process of examining currents trends inside and outside the college. We brought in a consultant on strategic planning from a Fortune 500 company to help us with the process . . . We tried to develop our capacities to anticipate problems in advance, to monitor our internal and external environments, and to be informed about the influences that were coming to bear on the college before they turned into problems for us.

In the eyes of many trustees, demographics and markets were among the most influential considerations. Hence, the more strategic boards initiated conversations and encouraged analytical studies about how their colleges could respond, for example, to "a more diverse work force of women and minorities" or to the prospect "we recognized a number of years ago . . .

that the market of high-school graduates was going to shrink." These boards often advanced their discussions through *information*. For instance, corporate executives on one board provided data from their own in-house studies as well as personal judgments of the problems and needs of the workplace. "When you pull these business leaders together and listen to what they have to say," stated one board chairman and CEO of a multinational computer company, "the board picks up very quickly and tries to translate this into 'What does this mean for the college?' The college listens well. . . . They view the community as their customer and watch the radar screen of their customers." In this case, the college's strategic response was to open an extremely successful downtown campus easily accessible to "the largest concentration of working adults."

Other boards advanced strategy by stimulating *insight*, a difficult talent to define or cultivate. Somehow, insightful boards were able to discern, capture, and interpret often faint and distant signals. "How did we see ahead?" asked one trustee rhetorically. "Like all deliberative matters, some studies were made in a formal way. One or two individuals have a flash of judgment and get in position to encourage their ideas, and some are just forced on you. Even in businesses with good reputations for planning, so much of it is ad hoc."

Whatever the particular ingredients of insight, some examples are instructive. One board long anticipated the need to acquire additional land that could be developed into a research and industrial park that would generate income, and the board also realized that a major thoroughfare that bisected the campus had to be rerouted to create a physically, aesthetically, and symbolically unified college. Ever mindful of these needs, the board "seized the opportunity" when the political climate and personal relationships between the board and the local government shifted favorably. The board was at the ready and acted quickly. In another case a board, able to foresee a potential struggle a few years ahead with an alumni booster organization, "moved to prevent future conflict by stepping in early and inviting the alumni group to join our resources committee and to work together on setting priorities and raising funds. That worked out really well."

Other boards contributed through *inquiry*. Concerned about a projected decline in high school graduates in the college's recruitment region, one strategic board initiated a series of discussions with the president about "better ways to market to attract a broader range of students by offering a few new programs." That approach succeeded so well that "it meant some difficult choices regarding limiting growth and curtailing enrollment in several areas. But we could see that procrastination would harm us more." In sum, strategic boards scanned and grasped the external environment, directed the board's attention to future-oriented issues and longer-term trends, and then worked closely with the president to identify the institutional implications and appropriate organizational actions.

Effective boards monitored the college's internal environment with a similar attentiveness. Although the specific topics differed, there was a common tendency to focus on the horizon rather than the foreground and to anticipate rather than react. On issues as dissimilar as divestment, maintenance, or presidential performance, effective boards were both action-oriented *and* future-oriented. Stated another way, boards perceptive enough to foresee tendencies and trajectories were able to act early enough to stem unfavorable trends. Consider these three comments, all by trustees of exemplary boards.

> Well, we could see a problem coming with the condition of the old dormitories. . . . It doesn't pay to wait and let things get really bad before you act. The board worked up a plan to look at all our dormitory needs and decide where to renovate and where to rebuild. We now have some very nice facilities for our students. Coming out of these experiences we also realized that it was not good business to wait until we needed to do some work to find the money to support it. So now we're setting up a separate fund that will provide income to handle maintenance and replacement needs as they arise.

> We could see problems coming with the previous president. He was already providing plenty of signals that he wouldn't work out here, but it's really difficult to gear yourself up to that sort of struggle. But we told ourselves that not acting would just make things worse, so we bit the bullet and faced the issue.

> We did not want to let the issue of divestment simmer. . . . There were incidents at other schools, and we wanted to make sure that that didn't happen here.

These effective boards had the capacity to project scenarios over an extended time horizon and to determine through that process whether more immediate actions were necessary and appropriate.

Ineffective boards did not exhibit such skills. Indeed, some of members of these boards were unable to recall *any* occasion where the trustees anticipated a problem before the matter became urgent. "No, sad to say, I can't think of a single one." Or the response was distinctly nonstrategic: "We saw the enrollment declines and hired a recruiter, but she didn't work out well. I'm not sure why." Or the board's action was too little, too late:

> We didn't think we'd ever outgrow our space, but we weren't looking very far out or ahead. By the time we realized what was happening to the population and the economy in this area, everybody else had seen it too and land prices were way up. We were just late in discovering the necessity of planning for the future.

It is difficult to understand why some boards were so ill-equipped to concentrate on strategy and anticipate potential difficulties. Certainly the failure of these boards to approach matters analytically (see chapter 4) contributed to their problem. In large part, though, the answer may rest with a related skill we addressed in chapter 2, the capacity to create an environment where board members are encouraged to raise questions, doubts, and concerns. And while our earlier reference to the value of an open and inquisitive environment concerned conversations about the board's internal mode of operation, the principle can be applied to its governance responsibilities as well. Boards cannot be strategic or anticipatory if the dominant norms discourage them from confronting problems squarely. Under those circumstances, minor difficulties can fester and develop into substantial crises. A custom of not-so-benign neglect was noted, for example, by several members of one especially ineffective board.

> We avoided the issue until the decision was inescapable. Then we covered it up as quickly as possible.

> Mostly, it seems that the board tries to bury such issues, avoid them at all costs, and try not to face or deal with them. When finally they break out, there is a bad feeling all around, but that is buried quickly too.

The perhaps simple yet essential lesson to be learned from effective boards on this score was encapsulated well by the former chairman of a strong board: "Effective board leadership is the result of many things such as . . . recognizing problems early and facing them together."

We should add one postscript about boards that attempted to envision and shape institutional direction. The process entailed some risks. Sometimes actions that appear to be prudent over the long run can be unpopular or uncomfortable in the short run. For example, the decision by one board to purchase, and thus remove from the local tax rolls, additional land rankled some area residents. Nevertheless, that board firmly believed that the acquisition was essential to the long-term economic health of the college and the community and thus worth the immediate criticisms. In another instance, a board approved a doctorate in education for school administrators at a time when "conventional wisdom said there was no market." That program is now oversubscribed. "The college takes risks," the board's chairman declared. "This board does not believe in a hidebound condition."

Effective boards, then, seemed more inclined to take sensible risks and to accept responsibility and, on occasion, criticism for such decisions. Thus, the chairman of an effective board noted about a new alcohol policy that had been initially unpopular with some students, "We didn't hide from it, even though it wasn't a particularly pleasant issue. We acted like real stewards of the college." In other words, stronger boards realized that a vital part of their governance role was to assume risk *and* responsibility.

SUGGESTIONS

Shortly, we will describe three methods that boards can use to strengthen their strategic capabilities. These measures will help the typical or conventional nonprofit board to focus on strategic, institutional priorities. First, however, we want to note a more radical alternative.[1]

Convinced that hospitals can no longer function effectively with a traditional lay board of trustees, Delbecq and Gill (1988) suggested that the new role of a board should be as a "strategic think tank" for the CEO. Decision rules at board meetings would be "non-consensual" and the CEO would retain "implementation prerogatives and responsibilities" (p. 32). The large, voluntary lay board would be replaced by a board comprised of a small number of compensated experts in health care, perhaps buttressed by an auxiliary board of community supporters to assist with development and public relations. Moreover, the new "expert" board would essentially be advisory to the CEO and serve as a "challenge to organizational tunnel vision. . . . The essential function of the strategic board would be to support, counsel, stimulate, and evaluate the strategy which the CEO has responsibility to implement." In this new order of things, board agendas would concentrate on "environmental conditions and trends, current and potential markets, and other strategic concerns" (p. 32).

While the model, and certainly the goals, expounded by Delbecq and Gill have some appeal, such a dramatic departure from tradition may not be necessary for colleges, universities, and many other nonprofits to ensure that boards focus on organizational strategy and the institution's long term welfare. We offer three less drastic recommendations that should help channel a board's attention toward issues of some magnitude to the organization.

Establish priorities and work plans for the board and its committees. On the assumption that a general consensus exists about institutional mission and purpose, trustees next need to understand the relationship between the organization's overall "game plan" and the board's specific roles and responsibilities. As a first step in that process, the board might ask the president for a concise "memorandum of strategy" that answers the question: "What is your vision for the future of this institution and how do you expect to achieve it?" (Wood, 1984, p. 20). In response, the CEO paints with broad strokes a portrait of the years ahead that highlights central themes, values, initiatives, and strategies. We do not mean to suggest that the president should develop a vision statement singlehandedly. To the contrary, the CEO should periodically distill for the board the essence of a collaboratively constructed vision.

Once discussed, modified, and embraced by the board, the memoran-

---

[1] Portions of this section are adapted from R. Chait and B. Taylor, "Charting the Territory of Non-Profit Boards," *Harvard Business Review*, 67 (1), 44–54.

dum provides a strategic perspective on organizational direction and a "continuous agenda"[2] for the board. The document should also serve as a guide for trustees and senior managers to develop a work plan for each of the board's committees. Surprisingly few boards and even fewer board committees have an *annual calendar* that explicitly links the work of the board or trustee committees to the organization's strategic priorities. Such integrated work plans assist the board as a whole and its committees to set and pursue relevant priorities and to establish direct connections between their efforts and the college's goals. As the president and chair share each committee's plan with all board members, everyone has a better sense of how the various pieces fit together. To go a step further, nonconfidential elements of the plan could be shared with the campus community at large to enable others to better understand the board's responsibilities, concerns, and directions.

There are several other procedures that could be adopted to harness and focus the board's energies on strategic priorities:

- Items on board and committee agendas might be prioritized with the most important issues considered first, rather than toward the end of the meeting when trustees may feel depleted or rushed.

- A committee chair or staff liaison might suggest time guidelines or limits for each item as a function of its relative importance.

- Board meetings might begin with a presidential overview of the major topics under discussion and the linkages among the agendas of the various trustee committees.

- The appropriate administrative officer could provide a written preface to each major policy issue that places the matter at hand clearly within the larger context of corporate strategy. The preface would explain "Why this issue now comes to the board" and "How it relates to our 'continuous agenda.' "

- Senior managers can furnish in advance a list of questions for trustees to contemplate as a way to frame the discussion and to direct attention to those areas where the staff most needs the board's guidance.

- The board can reserve an hour or two at each of its meetings for the sole purpose of ensuring that the president has a chance to discuss whatever is uppermost in his or her mind.

- A committee's work plan and the board's 'continuous agenda' can be prominently displayed on newsprint or posterboard at each of its meet-

---

[2] This term was suggested in a conversation with Richard Umbdenstock, a consultant to hospital boards, based in Spokane, Washington.

ings as a visible reminder of the board's role, responsibilities, and priorities.

- The board can agree to operate with a "consent agenda" whereby the executive committee lists a series of actions or decisions that will be authorized on items judged to be of minor significance *unless* a trustee requests that the issue be discussed by the whole board.

Establish a "governance information system." To govern knowledgeably and effectively boards need *governance* information. Patton and Baker argued that "Even the most independent directors will be little more than rubber stamps if they're not provided with all the information needed to make intelligent decisions" (1987, p. 12). Too often, however, presidents bury boards beneath a mountain of irrelevant *management* or operational information, either as part of a well-intentioned effort to ensure that the board has "all the facts" or, more deviously, to divert the trustees' attention from important policy matters. Whatever the motive, the quality of trusteeship suffers as a result of too much of the wrong kind of information.

Presented with management information, dutiful trustees try to digest the data and delve into administrative matters. Why would anyone expect trustees to behave differently? Provide a board, for instance, with a line-item budget and almost certainly a few trustees will start to question various expense items. On the other hand, a board presented with information on the relationship between declared priorities and the reallocation of resources will be more apt to discuss matters of strategy. Hence, a board may wish to establish a governance information system (GIS).

Governance information has four essential properties (Butler, undated). These are:

1. *Strategic*. The data and performance indicators provided to the board are directly related to issues of corporate strategy.

2. *Normative*. Performance data are displayed for the board against norms, targets, and anticipated results, so that trustees can readily compare actual performance to historical trends, "industry" standards, and institutional expectations.

3. *Selective*. Trustees routinely receive only that information necessary to exercise proper oversight, to monitor institutional and management performance, and to prompt board action.

4. *Graphic*. Whenever possible, data are displayed in graphic formats that communicate directly and succinctly.

The procedures to develop a GIS are fairly straightforward. The board and senior managers need to determine together what information trustees need, how often, and in what format to govern the institution. A retreat, perhaps with an outside expert, affords an opportune occasion to ask the rarely asked question, "Why do we need this information?" After the board agrees on what information it needs, management translates that decision into data requirements—the content, format, and frequency of reports the administration must provide to the trustees. From time to time the board as a whole and each trustee committee could review and, as necessary, modify the GIS.

Fortunately for colleges and universities, the Association of Governing Boards developed a superb handbook titled *Strategic Decision Making: Key Questions and Indicators for Trustees* (1987) that covers ten "critical decision areas" from financial, academic, and student affairs to intercollegiate athletics and institutional advancement. (Butler [undated] provides similar guidance for hospital boards.) With the AGB volume as a guide, boards can easily establish an information calendar and a systematic procedure that will furnish pertinent data in a timely fashion. For example, a board might elect to receive reports on student enrollments, freshman profiles, graduation rates, and career placement each fall. Likewise a board might decide that information about tenure recommendations should focus less on individuals' professional qualifications, a province of the faculty and administration, and more on the relationship of the proposed actions to program priorities, budgetary parameters, and affirmative action goals.

A GIS offers a number of ancillary benefits to the board. First, the trustees' deliberations about their information needs will, in and of themselves, illuminate self-perceptions about the board's roles and stimulate fruitful discussions with the staff about appropriate divisions of authority, responsibility, and accountability. *By deciding together what data it needs to govern, a board will better understand just what it thinks governing means.*[3] Second, a common information base should help knit the board together and diminish the prospects of an inner circle armed with "inside information." Third, the system should reduce and mediate requests to the administration from individual trustees for information unrelated to the board's role and spheres of concern. Finally, a GIS provides a structure of knowledge about board functions that can serve as a very useful device to orient new trustees.

Robert Mueller, former board chairman of Arthur D. Little, Inc., and an expert on corporate boards, once observed at a seminar on governance that boards ironically have the most information about issues of the narrowest

---

[3] This process of thinking and learning by acting mirrors Weick's observation about how managers actually think: "Thinking is inseparably woven into and occurs simultaneously with action. . . . action incorporates thinking and . . . thinking occurs in a context of action" (1983, p. 222).

scope and, conversely, they have the least information about matters of the broadest significance. A governance information system alone cannot right that imbalance, but it will help considerably.

Monitor or "map" allocation of the board's attention. Just before or shortly after the end of the fiscal year, trustees and managers normally review how the organization's money was spent. In the same spirit, these groups should review how the *board's time* was spent. Both are precious resources that could, unless monitored carefully, be squandered on low priorities.

We have developed a framework that trustees can use to monitor allocation of the board's attention. Building on the observation in chapter 2 that effective boards seek feedback on their own performance, boards should assess whether their time as trustees was devoted to significant matters. By doing so, boards reduce the probability of reflexively and unconsciously dwelling on operational details to the neglect of strategic priorities.

This approach challenges a traditional tenet of trusteeship: that the board sets policies which the administration implements. Such a simple dichotomy obscures the ambiguities and complexities inherent in the governance process. There are simply too many circumstances that warrant trustee involvement in "administration." For example, there are cases where trustees have valuable, specialized knowledge to contribute, especially—though not exclusively—in the financial domain. Board members may have to be enlisted to lobby, to raise money, to sway public opinion, or to otherwise influence events in the external environment. Or trustees may be asked to open doors to corporations, cultural organizations, or government. To suggest on the other side of the equation that presidents and senior managers are not partners to policy development would be equally naive and ill-advised.

A more instructive approach, we believe, recognizes that there are *levels* of policy and *phases* of policy development and that the roles of the board and the administration shift among them accordingly. We will briefly describe these aspects of policy and then present a "map" that can be used to chart and analyze a board's allocation of attention.

Hodgetts and Wortman (1975) identified six *levels* of policy to which we have appended parenthetically some illustrative examples.

1. MAJOR POLICIES. Fundamental issues of mission or business definition, typically involving questions of institutional direction, values, priorities and principles. (Add graduate education, discontinue church affiliation, go co-ed)

2. SECONDARY POLICIES. Questions of primary clientele, types of services, delivery systems that may focus on relationship of programs and departments to overall mission. (Add new academic department,

establish educational television station, substantially revise admissions criteria)

3. FUNCTIONAL POLICIES. Concerns of major operational areas; for example, planning, budgeting, finance, marketing, and personnel. (Budget approval process, investment policies, setting tuition and overhead rates)

4. MINOR POLICIES. Decisions that govern day-to-day practices. (Participation in United Way campaign, selection of contractors, intercollegiate athletic schedule)

5. STANDARD OPERATING PROCEDURES. Mechanisms and procedures to handle routine transactions and normal operations—matters of form, process, method, and application of other policies. (Grade appeals, student discipline, sabbatical requests)

6. RULES. Regulations that guide or prescribe everyday conduct. (Parking, smoking, library fines, dormitory visitation)

These policy levels should not be viewed as a rigid hierarchy, and a board need not scientifically classify every item on its agenda. Instead, when a matter does come before the board, the trustees should have some sense of the issue's place on the policy spectrum. Is this a higher level policy matter? If not, is there some reason why the topic has been placed on the agenda? The answer may be that the subject has implications for higher level policies. If so, those implications should be made the explicit focus of attention. As a rule, the board should devote little energy to lower level policy decision and considerable energy to higher level policy decisions.

Along with the level of policy, the board must be alert to the *phases* of policy development. Trustees have a different role to play at each stage of this process. The four phases of policy development and the board's role at each stage are as follows:

1. DEFINE POLICY OBJECTIVES. Articulation of the intended purposes to be achieved by a policy. The board has an early, active role, usually through formal and informal conversations with the president and senior officers. Occasionally, the board may initiate a policy objective to be attained.

2. FORMULATE THE POLICY STATEMENT. Drafting of a document that meets the stated aims. The administration manages the process, drafts the policy, and keeps the board apprised as preferred options emerge. The board ensures that the policy meets the objectives, that the process of consultation is suitable, and that the criteria for evaluation are appropriate. Trustees may raise questions or express reservations, but the board must resist the temptation to rewrite policy rec-

ommendations. Boards are more effective as questioners and reactors than as editors. State the objection, articulate the concern, offer the suggestion, and then direct the administration to craft the proper language.

3. IMPLEMENT THE POLICY. The board participates selectively when involvement provides an important chance to improve communication with key constituents, conduct a "spot check," learn about the organization, or to exploit the board's expertise or influence. Otherwise, the administration manages day-to-day policy execution.

4. MONITOR THE POLICY. For higher level policies, the board and president establish a time line or trip wires that trigger an evaluation of the policy's effects. When the time arrives, the CEO briefs the board thoroughly about the policy's consequences. For midlevel policies, the CEO occasionally reports on the policy's impact and for lower level polices, the CEO simply assures the board that evaluations occur. In all cases, management designs and conducts the assessment, analyzes the results, and suggests any policy changes.

How do these six policy levels and four stages of policy development work together to define a board's role and harness the trustees' energies? Figure 6–1 provides an "attention map" on which the board's major activities can be plotted against both levels and phases of policy. Every year or so, each trustee could be asked to rank-order the issues that have most occupied the board. Then markers could be drawn on the map at places that best reflect the policy level and the phase(s) of policy development that involved the board. Boards with a penchant for precision could prorate their markers to represent the relative time an issue commanded. The goal, however, is not to be needlessly elaborate; rather, it is to provide in sharp relief a visual representation of where the board's attention has been directed with respect to levels and phases of policy. The board can then assess whether its time was well budgeted and its energy well spent.

In the main, the markers for effective boards should congregate in the upper left-hand portion of Domain 1, since higher level policy objectives and statements are, almost by definition, inextricably coupled with an institution's strategic priorities. Some markers may be scattered elsewhere in Domain 1 as reflections of the board's episodic participation in implementing and monitoring important policies. Effective boards pay less attention to developing midlevel policy objectives and statements and expend little effort on their implementation. Therefore, Domain 2 should not be especially dense and the relatively few markers within that segment should be skewed toward the upper left-hand corner. Domain 3 should be almost empty, as effective boards devote almost no attention to any phase of lower level policy development or implementation.

FIGURE 6–1   Focus of Board's Attention

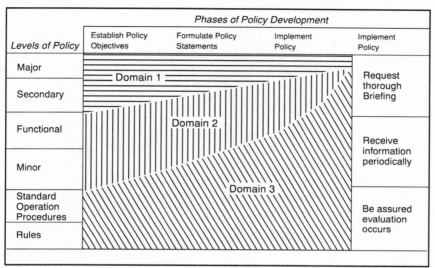

Were Domain 3 the most heavily populated, then the likelihood that the board was being effective and strategic would be questionable. Boards with a pattern weighted toward the lower right hand portion of the map must (re)examine their performance and consciously redirect their energies toward major policies and strategic priorities.

Conclusion. No approach to governance can guarantee that a board will always be effective. On the other hand, we believe that the probability of success will increase significantly if trustees recognize that the board's role varies depending on the level of policy under consideration and the phase of the policy development cycle.

There are legitimate circumstances—and we have described some—where a board might venture more deeply into the realm of lower level policies or participate more directly in the later stages of policy development. Alert to that possibility, we have presented a dynamic and contingent model. The board must be elastic, able to stretch and adapt as circumstances warrant. Yet, at the same time, it must be sufficiently resilient, disciplined, and self-aware to refocus its attention on higher priorities when more normal conditions return.

Boards with priority-driven work plans, a governance information system, and sensitivity to the general level and phase of policy development will be better able to target and pursue the key, long-term strategic questions that merit trustees' attention. They will be better prepared to focus their thinking on questions truly crucial to the organization's future.

Without these aids, boards are prone to wander into extensive consideration of insignificant issues merely because information was available or because someone placed the matter on the trustees' agenda. Almost imperceptibly, such boards slip into a morass of minutiae from which few escape easily. Their members are condemned to attend boring meetings while their institutions drift or, worse, sink on an even keel.

DISCUSSION QUESTIONS AND EXERCISES

1. Ask each trustee to list the institution's three to five top priorities for the next five years. Collate the responses to see whether a general consensus exists. If so, ask each board committee, along with the appropriate senior staff, to develop a priority-driven work plan for at least the next twelve months. If no consensus is obtained, the president and chair need to lead a discussion to clarify strategic priorities and resolve differences.

2. To highlight the need to monitor progress, ask the board to identify the institution's top three to five priorities five years ago. To what degree were those priorities attained? Where is the evidence? What are the implications for monitoring current priorities?

3. As a way to help envision the future, each trustee and senior administrator might be asked to write a one- or two-sentence response to each of the following questions. (1) What *is likely* to be most different about this institution in ten years? (2) What do you *wish* would be most different about this institution in ten years? (3) What change in the external environment over the next ten years do you think will most directly affect this institution and in what way? (4) What would be the most visible, tangible sign of this board's success ten years from today? For a lighter touch, the exercise could be treated as a "time capsule," with the collated responses revealed to the board (or even the entire campus community) and then sealed in an envelope to be opened at a board meeting or retreat ten years hence.

4. Discuss an occasion when the board was able to anticipate a problem and act before the issue became urgent or critical. Try to identify the factors that most enabled the board to be farsighted. Are there any ways to build those factors permanently into the board's activity patterns?

5. Using the AGB *Strategic Decision Making* handbook as a guide, ask each board committee (along with the staff liaisons) to determine the most important performance indicators to monitor, and then develop with the administration the appropriate components of a governance information system.

6. As described earlier in this chapter, chart the board's attention patterns on a "map" that plots levels of policy and phases of policy development. Is the board satisfied with the results? What specific steps can the board take to devote more time and attention to higher level policy objectives and to strategic priorities?

7

What's A President
To Do?

THE PIVOTAL PARTNERSHIP

The preceding chapters focused largely on the competencies and behaviors of boards of trustees as discrete entities. This is not to suggest, however, that presidents are peripheral to board effectiveness. To the contrary, we included this chapter in a book otherwise directed at trustees precisely because the president can play a crucial role in encouraging, or undermining, effective board functioning.

Practitioners and scholars alike often describe the board-president relationship as a partnership based on mutual support and trust. But the relationship is paradoxical. Technically, the board is the president's employer, yet trustees usually acknowledge the president as the board's de facto leader. This mutual dependence may more accurately be described as an "exchange relationship" (Blau, 1986) in which the board and president rely on each other to supply the information, credibility, and support that enables them to perform their respective roles effectively. The more successful the board, the more complex and multifaceted the board-president exchange tends to be.

For a president, the board and its members can function as employers, critics, friends, counselors, and confidantes. For a board, the president can be a teacher, leader, employee, colleague, and advisor. Among the less effective boards we studied, presidents and boards frequently viewed each other in unidimensional terms. The board considered the president exclusively as an employee or as the undisputed "king" of the college, whereas the president regarded the board solely as uninformed critics or unwavering members of a fan club.

The mutual understanding between board and president that characterized productive relationships was based on a fuller comprehension and appreciation of what each party can bring to the leadership of the institution, what each can contribute to the other, and what each needs from the other in order to perform well. As Drucker (1990, p. 10) observed:

> Nonprofits waste uncounted hours debating who is superior and who is subordinate—board or executive officer. The answer is that they must be colleagues. Each has a different part, but together they share the play. Their tasks are complementary. Thus, each has to ask, What do I owe the other? not—as board and executive officers still tend to do—What does the other owe me?

Trustees and presidents affiliated with effective boards did not attempt to translate these complexities into neat job descriptions that specified exactly what the board and president would do in every possible situation. In reality, healthy relationships rested on shared understandings of general roles and mutual expectations that evolved and changed over time and that resulted from honest communication and an open acknowledgement of interdependence.

The preceding chapters raise two fundamental questions for presidents: Why should you want to assist your board to become more effective? And, what can you do to help the board develop its capabilities? The next two sections answer these questions respectively.

WHY SHOULD A PRESIDENT WANT AN EFFECTIVE BOARD?

At first blush, many presidents reject as irrational any activity aimed at empowering their board. What sane chief executive wants an energetic and informed board second-guessing the president's leadership and vision? And on the face of it, there seems to be little reason why a president should feel obliged to develop the board. The board's legal authority notwithstanding, in the eyes of most trustees the president occupies the more powerful position in the relationship.

Alderfer maintains that "in a variety of ways—both explicit and subtle—CEOs tell directors what they want, and they usually get it. Only in a crisis do directors depart from the CEO's expectations, and then they do so deliberately" (1986, p. 27). Trustees perceive the president as having greater power than the board because, among other factors, the president has more time, expertise, and information to offer to the institution, and therefore more control over board agendas, meetings, and decision-making processes. At least in the absence of crisis, boards tend to assume that they should support the president and take their cues from the CEO about what constitutes appropriate involvement in the organization's affairs. Trustee egos may figure in this acquiescence as well. Reluctant to reveal their own ignorance to fellow board members or to the president, many trustees often decide to keep quiet and follow the president's lead, rather than ask searching questions or suggest alternative courses of action (Lorsch, 1989, pp. 83–89).

The size of most independent college boards, thirty-two members on average (Taylor, 1988), also limits trustees' participation and their sense of authority and accountability. First, some trustees are inhibited by the board's size. "Do I really have something to say that thirty sharp people need to hear? Not too often, so I keep quiet," remarked one board member. Second, the perceived loss of dignity or credibility that results from expressing inappropriate or uninformed views increases with the number of people in the room. Finally, the larger the board, the less likely any one board member will feel a sense of individual responsibility (Patton and Baker, 1987, p. 10). As one member of a particularly ineffective board confessed, "My information is third-hand and I really have little idea what's going on or who is responsible. We're supposed to provide direction for the president, but I'm not sure we really do that." Even in the health care sector, where boards tend to be somewhat smaller, experts believed that "large trustee structures" created a dispersed sense of accountability among board members (Delbecq and Gill, 1988, p. 27).

For these reasons, among others, presidents may be able to reign supreme over a disengaged board. But what are the prices to be paid by the board and the president? The failure of boards to fulfill their governance responsibilities has at least two negative consequences. Boards that do not participate actively in making significant policy decisions lack the strategic institutional perspective necessary to true stewardship and thus depend by default on the president alone for this purpose. The members of one ineffective board, for instance, cited the president himself, rather than any aspect of the college's mission, history, or program as the institution's most distinctive characteristic. But when the president leaves a board like this one, the trustees frequently falter—just when the need for leadership is greatest. Second, many talented trustees lose patience and interest when the board does not deal with the most crucial questions facing the institution (Chait and Taylor, 1989, p. 44).

From a CEO's perspective, a passive board sometimes seems quite desirable. Hence, many presidents attempt to lull their boards into complacency and compliance. In the short run, presidents may welcome the latitude they gain from working with a submissive board. In fact, though, there are advantages over the longer term to a president who works to develop a better informed and more strategically focused board.

The loneliness of the college presidency has been well-documented. Discussions of leadership in higher education have observed that the president has no one to rely on, no one to talk to, and that he or she is out there all alone facing the demons that beset the institution (Kerr and Gade, 1986; Wood, 1984). The board plays one of three roles in the saga of the lonely presidency. First, board members may be so distanced from the college that they do not think very often about the president's situation nor are they particularly concerned about the pressures on the chief executive and the institution. Second, disengaged boards may view the president as a heroic figure for whom board support is superfluous. Or third, the board may have impossible expectations of the president and be hypercritical when the CEO fails to perform miracles on demand.

Some presidents in this study delighted in being perceived as lonely heros by their boards. But not all were comfortable in the role. A CEO who was held in very high regard by a relatively ineffective board said, "I wish I could make them into a board that would be harder on me and then support me in the decisions we make together." This president sensed what many successful chief executives know: CEOs need a source of objective advice, which is unlikely to come from faculty and staff, and of critical feedback, which subordinates in the administration are usually reluctant to provide. The catch is that uninformed and uncommitted boards are unlikely to provide insightful and constructive advice.

Efforts by presidents to constrain board authority or to discourage greater board involvement are risky and can backfire. For every president who "ruled" until retirement, informed observers can name many more who were eventually brought down by boards that grew intolerant and frustrated at being relegated to second-class status in the decision-making process. A member of an ineffective board that had seen several unsuccessful presidencies in the course of a few years remarked,

> I've served under three presidents—two of whom were defensive about the board and did not wish the board to be involved until the administration had made up its mind about what was to be done. In other words, a fait accompli. They didn't get the board involved early on in the decision-making process.

In Lorsch's words, "A successful CEO has to develop a rapport with the board. The ones than don't are in jeopardy" (1989, p. 89). Clearly, then, presidents have a deeply vested, personal interest in fostering boards that are engaged. Patton and Baker (1987, p. 12) suggested that a "CEO should want a strong board, not a compliant one, even if that goes against human nature," largely because informed and engaged boards are associated with more successful organizations. That finding, confirmed by our study, should be reason enough for presidents to invest in their boards' development. But we also discovered that when a president devoted considerable care and attention to educating, nurturing, and communicating with trustees, three interrelated benefits resulted. The board displayed: (1) a deeper understanding of the nature of academic leadership; (2) a greater appreciation of the president's role and circumstances; and (3) a heightened sense of attachment to the college.

There is not much disagreement or mystery about how a board wants to be treated by its CEO. Lorsch (1989, pp. 90–91) outlined succinctly the kinds of support corporate directors need from their presidents in order to participate meaningfully in organizational governance.

> Directors want a CEO who facilitates discussion without dominating or slanting it, who is open, who frequently encourages them to express their views, and who seeks their counsel. Most fundamentally, they want one who develops a rapport with them and demonstrates trust in them. Such a CEO doesn't flaunt power but invites the directors to help lead the company.

College trustees have similar expectations. Nevertheless, some campus CEOs halfheartedly and single-handedly attempted to inform and involve their boards. Rather than work over the long term to help the trustees themselves become committed to this idea, many presidents simply developed agenda, information packets, retreats, or educational programs without any substantial board participation. Not surprisingly, these initiatives did not have nearly the empowering effects as activities that resulted from direct board involvement.

College presidents associated with effective boards acted as true educators, helping to instill and facilitate the trustees' desire to learn more about their institution, the nature of the profession, and the roles and responsibilities of the board. Such efforts enabled the trustees of effective boards to be both more enlightened and more engrossed. Opportunities for a president to educate and engage trustees, and thus improve the board's performance, suffuse all six competencies of effective boards, as the following sections suggest.

WHAT CAN A PRESIDENT DO TO STRENGTHEN A BOARD'S PERFORMANCE?

I. The Contextual Dimension

Patton and Baker (1987, p. 13) noted about corporate boards that "over time, chief executives usually get the boards they want. The chief executive has by far the strongest voice in determining who's on the board. It may take a little time, but eventually the board is almost totally of the CEO's making." While presidents of public institutions clearly do not wield such power, presidents of independent colleges and universities often exert significant leverage over the selection process. In any case, the president's potential for influence extends far beyond selection, starting with orientation programs that can help new board members understand and take into account the specific institutional context that surrounds board decision making.

Trustee Selection. Among independent institutions, presidents sometimes exercise so much control over the trustee selection process that they can effectively compromise the board's authority to perpetuate itself. It is the president, after all, who is probably more willing to give time to the cultivation of prospective board members because no one has more to gain from attracting the right trustees. In fact, the president's role in recruiting trustees at independent colleges can be so deeply entrenched that at least one board chair reportedly "fears that a stronger trustee presence in recruitment might offend the president" (Wood 1985, p. 82).

Even if the president's recruitment efforts are fruitful, a CEO who does not work to involve the board in the selection process errs in several ways. First, the CEO forsakes an important opportunity to educate his or her board about the kinds of skills and perspectives the college needs among new trustees, given the board's current profile. Second, a discerning prospective trustee will probably want to (and probably should) meet and talk with a few board members before deciding whether to accept the appointment. Finally, there is some danger for the board and the institution if over the long run the president in effect owns the board. To the extent that trustees are too beholden to the president or too like-minded, the board may lose its capacity to think independently and analytically.

Like raising major gifts, trustee selection is a long-term process that begins with prospect identification, proceeds through cultivation, and culminates sometimes months or even years later in "the ask." Cultivation allows the parties to become acquainted at an unhurried pace and to decide whether or not their relationship has the capacity to endure. Rather than hastily ask an apparently attractive candidate to join the board, presidents and boards should first ask themselves some fundamental questions: What talents and traits do we need on this board at this time? What can this person contribute to the board *as a group*? What is the best way of approaching the candidate? How can we test his or her potential for commitment to our board and college?

Trustee Orientation. While 61 percent of all private colleges and universities reported that they provide formal orientation for new trustees (Taylor, 1988), few board members and presidents we interviewed seemed satisfied with the effort. Members of ineffective boards were likely to report that they had no orientation. Trustees of midrange boards and even some members of otherwise effective boards were apt to report that, while formal orientation was provided to new trustees, it was not entirely pertinent or useful. Board members and presidents most frequently invoked "osmosis" as the term that best described the usual mode of learning about the trustee's role.

In the absence of a well-designed orientation program, new trustees are less likely to be socialized to the board's norms, behaviors, and expectations.

Yet, the socialization of new members is a crucial component of successful efforts to permanently install, or institutionalize, organizational values or significant changes. In a study of attempts to introduce substantial organizational change, Goodman and Dean (1982, p. 249) reported that "it is surprising that these organizations did not pay more attention to socialization of new members . . . given that all the organizational forms are very complicated in terms of operations, beliefs, and values." In addition, the authors concluded that when incumbent members of the organization explained the rationale for certain behaviors to newcomers, the very act of transmission reinforced "the existence (or institutionalization) of these behaviors" among *all* members of the organization (p. 248). Thus, presidents may wish to involve seasoned trustees in the orientation process as a way to sustain their commitment as well.

Unfortunately, as we noted in chapter 1, most orientation programs are confined to describing the board's structure and processes and reviewing the college's administrative organization. Discussions of the role of the trustee and the board, particularly as stewards of the college's history, mission, and values, were conspicuously absent. Among the few exceptions, the president of one college met individually with each new trustee to explain the board's expectations, to describe the generic aspects of academic governance, and to underscore what was singular about *this* college and *its* conception of trusteeship.

In order to begin developing the new trustees' sense of institutional context, a president should consider providing the following written information prior to the orientation session:

1. Profiles of fellow board members that give the new trustee some idea of what others on the board are like as people: not only their education, occupation, and the usual resumé items, but also information about family, personal interests and commitments, the member's association with the college, and perhaps a one- or two-sentence statement from each trustee about why he or she joined the board.

2. *Succinct* information about board bylaws and structure; an abstract of major policy decisions by the board in recent years; an overview of the academic program, the faculty, student body, and administrative organization; an executive summary of any strategic or long-range plans; and an interpretation of key financial statements. The emphasis is on succinct. Presidents should avoid overwhelming new appointees with reams of operational data that will probably do more to confuse than illuminate a newcomer's understanding of the college's context and the challenges it faces.

3. Any available material that reveals the culture and values of the college: a written history or visual time line, newspaper clippings about

institutional achievements, profiles of outstanding faculty and students, and vignettes that capture the essence of the college's character.

It is well worth the effort to develop such resources for long-term use. Interviews with alumni and emeritus faculty, staff, and trustees about the college's past or about its effect on their lives can be preserved in print or on video tape. These should not be Madison Avenue productions that depict the college as a perfect place. The record should include setbacks as well as successes and faults as well as virtues; the tone should be unassuming and straightforward.

A one-day orientation program might include:

- An overview by the president or board chair of the orientation program and its purposes.

- A discussion involving the president, one or more incumbent trustees, a senior academic officer, a faculty leader or two, and the new trustee(s) about the college's mission, programs, and constituents. The discussion should move beyond standard catalogue copy to stress the features that distinguish this college from others that may look quite similar to an outsider.

- Conversations with faculty and students about the traditions of shared governance and about why and how it is practiced at this particular institution.

- A discussion involving the president, one or more incumbent trustees, and the new board member(s) about how the board does its work, the challenges it faces, and what it needs most from its new members. This should serve as a reiteration in greater detail of information provided during the cultivation process.

- A discussion with the president, one or two incumbent trustees, development and financial officers, and the new board member(s) about the college's financial affairs, physical plant, and resource needs. This discussion should emphasize the relationship between resources and the mission and priorities of the institution.

- If possible, some contact with a few "living legends"—an alumnus, emeritus trustee, or faculty member who embodies the college, its values, and its traditions.

- Social opportunities with a few students and faculty that enable the new trustee(s) to begin knowing campus constituents as individuals.

Faculty and staff participants in a trustee orientation should realize that this program may well be a board member's first (or certainly most recent) opportunity to judge the college's ability to educate. After all, orientation sessions *are* essentially educational activities. Consequently, the president might draw upon some of the institution's best teachers and teaching techniques to ensure that the orientation showcases the quality of education the college delivers.

II. The Educational Dimension

Continuing Board Development. Just as commencement speakers regularly remind students that graduation from college marks the *start* of a lifelong education, presidents must remind board members that orientation programs are an early point on the trustee's learning curve and that they represent only one component of the board's ongoing development. Presidents must ensure that board development is not limited to newcomers or to formal occasions such as orientations and retreats.

The president and senior administrators can incorporate into every board or committee agenda a short, fifteen- to thirty-minute educational segment on a matter of immediate relevance or long-term significance to the college and the trustees. Such briefings are good techniques to accustom trustees to board education and to gradually generate enthusiasm for activities, like retreats, that require more time and commitment. At the barest minimum, the CEO could relate at each board meeting an anecdote that encapsulates the college's essential values or distinctive characteristics. The central actors in the vignette could even be introduced to the board.

Regular communications from the president on institutional events, general higher education trends, and trustee responsibilities offer another simple but effective means to extend the board's knowledge base. A campus CEO can also provide board members with books (or more realistically, excerpts), pamphlets, or subscriptions to the *Chronicle of Higher Education* and *Change* magazine. Materials that place the board's deliberations in a larger context—national trends in tuition increases and student enrollments, innovative board practices, federal education policy—are most apt to be read. Finally, upon return from a conference or workshop, the president can briefly report to the board on the best ideas presented at that event. Through such efforts, individual board members stay informed about the college and the profession, and the president conveys to the trustees a concern for their continuing education.

Board Retreats. Many of the presidents and members of effective boards we interviewed mentioned the value of board retreats, both as a way to transmit substantive information to trustees and as a regular check on the board's processes and performance. One member of such a board remarked about a retreat designed to increase the board's knowledge of financial affairs that "not only did we learn a lot, but the retreat also raised the president's sights about financial issues and means of communicating more effectively with the board." In other words, while the ostensible purpose of this retreat was to educate the board, a side effect was increased knowledge on the part of the president about how to deal more constructively with the board. Because retreats tend to be intense and introspective, the president and the board are often challenged to rethink old assumptions and behavior patterns.

The general purposes of a retreat typically include one or more of the following:

1. To strengthen board performance through a review of governance processes and the board's roles and responsibilities.

2. To establish priorities for the board and to identify strategies to achieve those goals.

3. To enhance collegiality and working relationships among trustees and between the board and president.

4. To determine next steps in board development and in the implementation of an overall action plan.

The pathway to a successful retreat begins with broad consensus among trustees to have the retreat and to be present for the entire program. The board should consider the general purposes of the retreat, the board's perceived needs, possible topics to be covered, and whether or not to use an outside facilitator. The advantages a skilled facilitator can bring to the retreat include objectivity, knowledge of effective board operations, and experience as a moderator. The trustees' commitment to the retreat should be manifested in a formal board resolution.

In an excellent book on developing and conducting board retreats, Savage emphasized throughout that "every step the board takes in this [retreat] process is a model of how the board should normally operate" (1982, p. 13). That is, what may look like an elaborate effort to seek board input about the retreat actually reinforces the authority, accountability, and commitment of trustees. Consequently, the president should be careful to engage the board in the process from the outset.

Along with the board chair and perhaps the committee on trusteeship, the president can build consensus for the retreat by talking with individual trustees, gathering information about successful retreats held by boards of peer institutions, contacting organizations and consultants experienced in facilitating retreats, and reviewing literature that describes the purposes and formats of board retreats.

Once a board agrees to a retreat, it should appoint a small agenda committee that includes the president, the chair of the committee on trusteeship, and one or two other board members to plan the event and to guide any follow-up activities. Committee members should talk informally with all other board members to make certain that development of the agenda takes into account each trustee's perspectives and priorities. The committee should then meet (along with the facilitator, if there is one) to plan the program's content and format and to draft an agenda to be circulated among the board for comment and revisions.

Concurrently, trustees can be asked to complete anonymously one of several questionnaires on board and trustee performance. (See chapter 2 for specific instruments.) The results of such surveys, which should be collated and distributed to the trustees a week or more before the retreat, can help pinpoint the board's strengths and weaknesses as perceived by the board. Attention to these data can also help ensure that the retreat meets the board's specific needs.

If at all possible, the agenda committee should select a site for the retreat removed from the campus and conducive to informal yet intense activity. An overnight stay vastly increases the opportunities for social interaction and individual reflection. The agenda should maximize open discussion, widespread participation, and an action orientation. There should be a balance between plenary discussion and small group work sessions. Small group discussions should be guided by concrete, action-oriented questions drafted by the agenda committee prior to the retreat and modified as needed at the retreat. Each group session should result in an oral summary and a written set of recommendations and conclusions that take the form of a "game plan" for action subsequent to the retreat.

Within a few weeks after the retreat, the agenda committee should prepare a written report that captures the "headlines" of the various sessions, outlines the specific action steps to be taken over the next several months, and designates the committees or individuals responsible for monitoring progress. The report should be circulated among the trustees for comments and corrections and ultimately adopted formally by the board.

III. The Interpersonal Dimension

Especially on larger boards that meet infrequently, service as a trustee can be a rather impersonal experience. Whatever one's relationship to the college, many trustees have little interaction *with one another* and thus feel little connection to one another. The president (and the board chair), therefore, has to supply much of the "social glue" that helps the board to be a more cohesive and more productive group. A president can take a variety of actions to enhance relationships among board members and between the board and the chief executive. Some are designed to keep trustees abreast of the college's affairs; others are intended to cultivate social and personal relationships.

Among the effective boards we studied, much of the contact outside of meetings concerned board business. Several CEOs, for instance, would write or call trustees periodically to seek their counsel on possible responses to an emerging concern, to provide an update on an important college matter, or to see whether the trustee had any concerns or questions the president could address. Some presidents distributed to all board members every couple of months a brief newsletter that digested recent news about the college. From the trustees' perspective, though, many of the most valuable exchanges occurred one-on-one between board meetings by mail, over the telephone, or in person.

A good deal of contact among presidents and members of effective boards was informal and social in nature and depended on presidential involvement to succeed. Many presidents arranged dinners and receptions in conjunction with board meetings. Effective boards and their presidents saw opportunities of this sort as a virtual necessity. Among ineffective boards, time devoted to anything but official board business was frequently seen as wasteful and inefficient.

At dinners and social events for the entire board, the president should recognize, as a family might, any trustees' milestones such as birthdays, anniversaries, or promotions. In addition, if the board adopted some goals for itself, as we recommended in chapter 3, then the president could help foster an esprit de corps by charting the group's progress and by celebrating those achievements too. On a more intimate scale, a president might arrange for a few trustees with a common interest to dine together or to attend an event on campus together. Or the president could arrange "field trips" for board members to visit, for example, another college, a student internship site, or an archaeological dig supervised by a faculty member. Such excursions serve both social and educational functions for boards.

Communication and social interaction outside of formal board meetings pay several dividends. They strengthen the board's cohesiveness by helping trustees to know one another better. They solidify the personal relationship between the president and the board, which, in turn, bolsters the president's position as a board leader. And they help trustees to stay well informed about the college, as even in "social" settings, board issues are inevitably discussed. Taken together, these effects increase the level of satisfaction with the trustee experience and the members' commitment to the board and the college.

IV. The Analytical Dimension

Earlier chapters stressed the need for trustees to comprehend the complexities of their college's environment as well as the ambiguities and subtleties of the issues before the board. Very few boards can perform these tasks well without the president's assistance. Yet many CEOs mistakenly believe that trustees should be shielded from complexity. Some worry that a discussion of multiple options or the long-term consequences of a proposed action would unfairly burden board members or exceed the trustees' analytical capabilities. Others are reluctant to review for trustees the strengths and weaknesses of several alternatives for fear that the board will then regard the president as an indecisive leader. Our experience with effective boards suggests quite the opposite. They can weigh the most complex issues intelligently and creatively—and indeed welcome the opportunity to do so—*if* the president furnishes them with pertinent information and a supportive context for discussion.

Most of the approaches we described in chapter 4 for a board to become more analytical hinge in some way on the president, either as an initiator and facilitator of discussions or as a supplier of information and feedback. Most significant policy questions that a board tackles, such as tuition levels, faculty compensation, financial priorities, or curricular reforms, can and should be viewed from several perspectives. Unless the president sincerely and explicitly encourages the board to examine the matter through "multiple frames," trustees, especially on less effective boards, may reach a perfectly "rational" decision that completely overlooks, for example, the political or symbolic dimensions of the issue. Likewise, unless the president explains the viewpoints of various campus constituencies or allows the stakeholders to do so directly, the board may have little appreciation for the subtle (or not so subtle) consequences of the CEO's recommended course of action or a trustee's proposed amendment. If a controversy then ensues or if the board's decision produces adverse consequences that might have been illuminated by a more thorough analysis by the CEO and the board, the trustees may well feel shortchanged and ill-served by the president.

In a word, the president should initiate discussions by the board that expressly raise the trade-offs as viewed through multiple frames and from the perspectives of diverse constituencies. Presidents usually have considerable latitude to frame the scope of an issue and to direct the flow of the discussion. In the short run, the easier tack may be to simplify matters for the board, present an unambiguous solution to a complex problem, and call the question. In the long run, though, presidents (and colleges) would do better to harness the trustees' analytical skills on complicated and critical issues the institution must confront.

In practical terms, this means that presidents might: (1) ask the board to brainstorm about alternative solutions to a thorny problem; (2) invite members of various constituencies to confer with the board; (3) trace their own thinking and articulate their own doubts on a proposed action; (4) play the role of a stakeholder with a different perspective; (5) urge trustees to explore the potential downside of a recommendation; (6) openly praise constructive criticism from the board; and (7) encourage senior staff by example and direction to do likewise with board committees.

A president's efforts to stimulate trustees to think analytically can meet several objectives. First, the board will learn far more about the decision at hand and the overall institutional context than if the CEO only presents a single alternative without discussing the trade-offs, constituents' opinions, or the thought process that led to the president's recommendation. Much of this background information can then be brought to bear on issues the board deals with subsequently. Second, the board will develop and reinforce a pattern of thinking that can be applied to other decisions. Graduate professional schools purport to teach students how to think—like lawyers, doctors, or managers for example. In the same vein, CEOs of educational institutions can help board members learn how to think like trustees. As board members learn to focus on the long-term and to ferret out and analyze objectively the *governance* facets of complex policy questions, the president will receive better input and support that will improve the quality of institutional decisions and thereby strengthen both the college and the CEO's position.

V. The Political Dimension

We stressed, particularly in chapter 5, that effective boards regularly interact with the college's constituents and genuinely respect the legitimate roles of others in the governance process. Furthermore, we noted that the behaviors of strong and weak boards differed markedly on this dimension of effective trusteeship. Fortunately for presidents, CEOs can have a particularly significant impact on a board's performance in this area.

There are three common approaches to board contact with constituents, and each implies a role for the president. In the first, trustees and constituents interact directly with one another, and the president serves as a facilitator who organizes and orchestrates the contact. In the second, the board hears regularly from the president about constituents' views, but the chief executive functions as the board's sole source and interpreter of this information. In the third approach, the board neither has direct contact with constituents nor regular information from the president about constituents' concerns and priorities. In this instance, the president acts as a barrier or buffer to separate and "protect" the board from constituents, nominally so that the trustees can function as detached stewards unencumbered by internal organizational politics.

Among presidents working with effective boards, the role of facilitator was by far the most common. When we asked members of effective boards to describe how the board learned about stakeholders' views, almost invariably the responses depicted some kind of direct contact arranged by the president.

Some presidents, however, are adamantly opposed to contact between the board and anyone other than the chief executive, on the grounds that shared access to the board erodes presidential power. One student of leadership, a former college president himself, suggested that faculty and students not be allowed to attend board meetings or serve on board committees, as the CEO alone must be the board's window on the institution. Otherwise, the president's "mystique," "charisma," and influence will inevitably diminish (Fisher, 1984, pp. 163–171). Based on the case studies we conducted, this argument seems ill-founded and wrong-headed.

At a more mundane level, some presidents are apprehensive about trustee contact with stakeholders due to a legitimate concern that individual board members will champion the causes of the disaffected or misconstrue an extremist's opinion as representative of an entire constituency. Rather than "quarantine" trustees, a cure far worse than the disease, presidents might help the board develop guidelines that stress the trustee's responsibility to channel grapevine information and the pleadings of special interests through the CEO to the appropriate administrative officer or board committee. These guidelines, which should be part of the trustee's handbook and reviewed at orientations, should include instructions and examples that will help trustees to fulfill the spirit of the board's intentions.

To further reduce the likelihood of "end runs," the president might create more, not fewer, occasions for trustees and constituents to interact. The greater the structured opportunities to meet with board members, the less stakeholders will feel compelled to resort to extraordinary means outside established channels. Similarly, the more contacts the president arranges between trustees and constituents, the more board members will be exposed to a cross-section of viewpoints and thus better-equipped to spot extreme perspectives.

At the same time, presidents need to attend to the other side of the equation. CEOs must help members of the campus community understand that, while the board desires regular interaction with constituents, individual trustees have no more authority to promise or act on the board's behalf than a lone professor or a single student can act on behalf of the faculty or the student body.

Finally, as a practical matter, presidents would be naive to assume: (1) that trustees will not seek or at least allow contact with stakeholders, regardless of the CEO's wishes, or (2) that disaffected faculty, students, and alumni will defer to the president's desire to bar or limit their communication with the board. Since efforts to isolate board members from constituencies are both counterproductive to effective trusteeship and impractical, the question for presidents becomes not whether but how to facilitate the interaction.

The president should be central to all the techniques we suggested in chapter 5 to reinforce a board's relationship with stakeholders, especially those on campus. Furthermore, as the one person closely connected to each constituency, the president, with advice from other campus and board leaders, can best link together people, issues, and tasks. As the orchestrator of these efforts, the president has a significant opportunity to enhance the personal value trustees and constituents derive from interaction with one another, as well as the impact of such collaborations on decisions made by the board and college.

For example, we recommend the use of multiconstituent task forces that bring trustees together with faculty, students, and administrators to discuss an important problem before the institution and to propose a course of action. In this instance, the president (again, after consultation with others) is probably in the best position to place the specific issue(s) to be addressed within an institutional context, to draft a charge to the group, to have staff gather background information, and to develop the mechanism by which participants should be selected. The president's role would be essentially the same in planning a multiconstituency retreat or a combined meeting of parallel board and faculty (or student) committees.

The president must also ensure that classroom visitations by trustees or academic presentations to the board by members of the faculty are just as thoughtfully planned. What subject matter would be of greatest interest to a particular trustee? Would the trustee enjoy attending a seminar in a familiar field or a new one? What faculty members and students would find the presence of a trustee least disruptive? What topics and professors would most stimulate trustees in a seminar designed especially for board members? Can the material be brought to bear in some way on a question confronting the board?

A similarly careful effort to match people and interests should accompany the president's plans for social events that bring board members together with constituents. As an example, whether trustees and faculty dine together on campus, at the president's home, or at professors' homes, the president should compose the dinner groups in a way that yields a compatible mix and some common interests that are identified to the parties beforehand.

In all of these endeavors, whether for business or pleasure, the president has to be a bit of a "social engineer." On the other hand, the CEO's principal concern should be to facilitate interactions that are likely to be productive, informative, and enjoyable. The goal is *not* to insulate board members from perspectives contrary to the president's or to otherwise distort a trustee's understanding of constituents' opinions.

Lastly, we recommend in chapter 5 that boards periodically disseminate information to the campus community as a way to broaden avenues of communication and to alter any perceptions that the trustees are remote, faceless, do-nothing caretakers of the college. These communications may profile various board members, outline the trustees' goals for the year ahead, or summarize the board's accomplishments and disappointments in the year past. In reality, the president may have to prod the board to be more public and more communicative, and he or she may have to provide staff members to help draft such documents.

VI. The Strategic Dimension

In the treatise *Academic Strategy*, Keller (1983, p. 165) contends that "every institution needs to have a forcible champion of good management and planning. It should be the president." We agree. The chief executive should be the college's principal strategist, especially on matters of long-term consequence to the organization. The board should be among the CEO's key allies and supportive critics.

Chapter 6 detailed several tactics boards can employ to focus on strategic issues; most of these approaches depend heavily on the president for implementation. First and foremost, the president should articulate the college's basic corporate strategy or business definition. Toward that end, we recommend that the president furnish the board about once a year with a "memorandum of strategy" that synthesizes the ideas and aspirations of various stakeholders into a holistic vision for the institution and that outlines an action plan to fulfill that vision. While dramatic changes in the vision are unlikely from year to year, specific priorities and programmatic emphases may indeed shift over time. The CEO's annual memorandum should galvanize the board and convey the president's perceptions of the college's (and the board's) top priorities. Aided by senior staff, the president can then assist trustees to translate the overall strategy into annual work plans for the board, for trustee committees, and for special task forces that may be needed to address issues that cross the boundaries of more than one committee.

By and large, whatever the president determines to be important, trustees accept as important. To that extent, presidential decisions about what issues and information to present to trustees for discussion exert a powerful influence over the board's attention span. We recommended in chapter 6, therefore, that presidents and boards create a governance information system. This tool would enable a CEO, eager to concentrate the board's energies on matters of strategic consequence, to distribute and discuss timely progress reports on institutional priorities. The CEO might also request that an hour or so be set aside at the start or finish of each board meeting for a *conversation* about "the problems that keep the president awake at night." We are confident, based on the interviews we conducted, that the vast majority of board members would relish the chance to learn about, ponder, and discuss the questions uppermost in the president's mind.

Whatever the particular topics a president selects for board consideration, the nature of the discussion will be greatly affected by how the CEO frames the issues. A president can structure the discussion to favor strategic considerations or operational details. For example, a proposal to refurbish residence halls could be positioned exclusively as a matter of physical plant and capital improvements. Alternatively, the president could explain how the proposal relates to the college's strategic goal of increasing student retention, and why devoting resources to residence halls makes more sense than such alternatives as hiring academic tutors or offering more seminars and fewer large lecture classes. Similarly, if a trustee asks at a board meeting that the college investigate the steps required to establish a Phi Beta Kappa chapter on campus, the president could enlarge the scope of the discussion to encompass the objectives such a chapter might serve and what other or better options exist to recognize the achievements of academically gifted students.

Whenever possible, the CEO and senior administrators should plainly link recommendations or topics before the board to the college's fundamental mission, values, and strategic priorities. Discussion of this kind serves two aims. First, it brings the president and board back to fundamental strategies: Why are we here? What do we want this college to be? How can we get there? And second, it encourages the analytical thinking and mutual understanding within the board that underlie other dimensions of board effectiveness.

When presidents present trustees with strategic issues and relevant information for candid consideration, the consensus can sometimes run counter to the chief executive's preferences. We recounted in chapter 1 the experience of a midrange board whose members decided that the president's "vision statement" departed too radically from the institution's liberal arts tradition. While the president had clearly hoped for a different conclusion, he came to accept the logic of the board's view and even appeared to appreciate the trustees' nudges either to mount a stronger case for the proposed changes or to present a more moderate recommendation. Most presidents affiliated with effective boards seemed to understand that in a truly open process, the chief executive cannot always control the outcome. Moreover, most successful CEOs will acknowledge that an effective board can sometimes advance a better idea or at least save the president from a misstep.

The final suggestion we offered to strengthen a board's strategic capabilities was to increase the opportunities for feedback on the board's performance so that there are numerous occasions to detect and correct any drift toward trivia. On this score, presidents can serve as a powerful model by insisting that their own performance be reviewed by the board, whether formally or informally, regularly or intermittently. (For guidelines on presidential assessment, consult Kauffman, 1980, chapter 9; Kerr 1984, chapter 5; and Nason, 1980). When trustees see that the president eagerly seeks and profits from such feedback, the board will probably be more disposed to do likewise. And frankly, even if the board does not, presidents should still press for an evaluation by the board, if only for their own benefit.

CONCLUSION

Throughout the course of this study, we observed many presidents who helped their boards become more effective than they might otherwise have been. Conversely, we encountered some presidents who gave only lip service to board development and a few others who discouraged or impeded any efforts by their trustees to become better informed and more involved in the life of the institution.

These differences in the CEOs' attitudes and behaviors are significant because what the president chooses to do (or not do) can either facilitate or frustrate a board's desires and attempts to improve. Most trustees look to the president for clues about what constitutes appropriate and effective board behavior and for ideas and initiatives to strengthen the board's performance. As the board's performance improves, the president has greater reason in turn to look to the board for guidance and leadership. In a sense, then, successful presidents promote successful boards and vice versa. The interplay between the two gives each a place to go for support and advice and challenges each to reach toward higher levels of performance. "Nonprofits," Drucker concluded (1990, p.9),

> need both an effective board and an effective executive. Practically every non-profit will accept one or the other half of this assertion. But, a good many will not accept that both are needed. Yet, neither the board-dominated nor the executive-dominated nonprofit is likely to work well, let alone succeed in perpetuating itself beyond the tenure of an autocrat, whether that individual be board chairperson or executive officer.

We do not, however, want to leave the impression that effective boards and effective presidents are merely a proxy for one another. Rather, we mean to suggest that boards and presidents can improve either because of or in spite of each other. The former approach is easier and more probable, the latter is more difficult and less likely.

Presidents committed to enhancing the effectiveness of their board will see improvements both in the board and in their own relationships with trustees. Such efforts on the part of presidents strike us as one of the better ways that they can invest their time.

References

ALDERFER, C. (1986). The invisible director on corporate boards. *Harvard Business Review, 64*(6), 38–52.

ALEXANDER, J. The university and morality. *Journal of Higher Education, 57*, (5), 463–476.

ALLISON, G. (1971). *Essence of decision.* Boston: Little, Brown.

ANDERSON, R. (1983). *Finance and effectiveness: A study of college environments.* Princeton, NJ: Educational Testing Service.

ANDREWS, K. (1980). *The concept of corporate strategy* (rev. ed.). Homewood, IL: Richard D. Irwin.

ARGYRIS, C. (1976). *Increasing leadership effectiveness.* New York: John Wiley & Sons.

ASHFORD, S. (1989). Self-assessments in organizations. *Research in Organizational Behavior, 11*, 133–174.

ASSOCIATION OF GOVERNING BOARDS OF UNIVERSITIES AND COLLEGES (1985). *Self-study criteria for governing boards.* Washington, DC: Author.

ASSOCIATION OF GOVERNING BOARDS OF UNIVERSITIES AND COLLEGES (1986). *Composition of governing boards.* Washington, DC: Author.

ASSOCIATION OF GOVERNING BOARDS OF UNIVERSITIES AND COLLEGES (1986). *Self-study guidelines and criteria for governing boards of independent colleges and universities.* Washington, DC: Author.

ASSOCIATION OF GOVERNING BOARDS OF UNIVERSITIES AND COLLEGES (1987). *Strategic decision making: Key questions and indicators for trustees.* Washington, DC: Author.

ASSOCIATION OF GOVERNING BOARDS OF UNIVERSITIES AND COLLEGES (1988). *Results of a national survey on board characteristics, policies, and practices.* Washington, DC: Author.

BALDRIDGE, J. V., CURTIS, D., ECKER, G., & RILEY, G. (1978). *Policy making and effective leadership.* San Francisco: Jossey-Bass.

BELLAH, R., MADSEN, R., SULLIVAN, M., SWIDLER, A., & TIPTON, S. (1985). *Habits of the heart.* Berkeley, CA: University of California Press.

BENNIS, W., & NANUS, B. (1985). *Leaders: The strategies for taking charge.* New York: Harper & Row.

BENSIMON, E., NEUMANN, A., & BIRNBAUM, R. (1989). *Making sense of administrative leadership: The "L" word in higher education* (ASHE-ERIC Higher Education Report No. 1). Washington, DC: The George Washington University, School of Education and Human Development.

BERLINER, D. (1989). *Expert knowledge in the pedagogical domain.* Paper presented at the American Psychological Association, New Orleans.

BIRNBAUM, R. (1988). *How colleges work.* San Francisco: Jossey-Bass.

BLAU, P. M. (1986). *Exchange and power in social life* (rev. ed.). New Brunswick, NJ: Transaction.

BOLMAN, L., & DEAL, T. (1986). *Modern approaches to understanding and managing organizations.* San Francisco: Jossey-Bass.

BOYATZIS, R. (1982). *The competent manager: A model for effective performance.* New York: John Wiley & Sons.

BUTLER, L. (undated). *An information system for the hospital board.* Belmont, MA: The Cheswick Center.

CAMERON, K., & BILIMORIA, D. (1985). Assessing effectiveness in higher education. *The Review of Higher Education, 9*(1), 101–118.

CARVER, J. (1990). *Boards that Make a Difference.* San Francisco: Jossey-Bass.

CHAFFEE, E. (1984). Successful strategic management in small private colleges. *Journal of Higher Education, 55*(2), 212–241.

CHAIT, R. P. (1979). Academic management: What it should be. In L. Jones & R. Nowotny (Eds.), *Preparing for the new decade: New Directions in Higher Education* (Vol. 28). San Francisco: Jossey-Bass.

CHAIT, R. P. (1989). *Defining and monitoring the effectiveness of boards of trustees.* College Park, MD: University of Maryland, National Center for Postsecondary Governance and Finance.

CHAIT, R. P. (1990). The decade of trustees. In L. Jones & R. Nowotny (Eds.), *Agenda for the new decade: New Directions for Higher Education* (Vol. 70). San Francisco: Jossey-Bass.

CHAIT, R. P., & TAYLOR, B. E. (1987). *Evaluating boards of trustees: Theory and practice.* Paper presented at the Association for the Study of Higher Education, Baltimore.

CHAIT, R. P. & TAYLOR, B. E. (1989). Charting the territory of non-profit boards. *Harvard Business Review, 67* (1), 44–54.

CLARK, B. (1970). *The distinctive college: Antioch, Reed, and Swarthmore.* Chicago: Aldine.

COHEN, M., & MARCH, J. (1974). *Leadership and ambiguity: The American college president.* New York: McGraw-Hill.

COPE, R. (1987). *Opportunity from strength: Strategic planning clarified with case examples*. Washington, DC: The George Washington University, Association for the Study of Higher Education.

DEAL, T., & KENNEDY, A. (1982). *Corporate cultures: The rites and rituals of corporate life*. Reading, MA: Addison-Wesley.

DELBECQ, A., & GILL, S. (1988). Developing strategic direction for governing boards. *Hospital & Health Services Administration*, 33(1), 25–35. Dill, D. (1982). The management of academic culture: Notes on the management of meaning and social integration. *Higher Education, 11*, 303–320.

DRUCKER, P. (1989). What business can learn from nonprofits. *Harvard Business Review, 67*(4), 88–93.

DRUCKER, P. (1990). Lessons for successful nonprofit governance. *Nonprofit Management & Leadership, 1*(1), 7–13.

FISHER, J. L. (1984). *The power of the presidency*. New York: American Council on Education/MacMillan.

FISHER, R. & BROWN, S. (1988). *Getting together: Building a relationship that gets to yes*. Boston: Houghton-Mifflin.

FLANAGAN, J. (1954). The critical incident technique. *Psychological Bulletin, 51*(4), 327–358.

GOODMAN, P. & DEAN, J. (1982). Creating long-term organizational change. In P. Goodman & Associates, *Change in organizations* (226–279). San Francisco: Jossey-Bass.

HACKMAN, J. R., & WALTON, R. (1986). Leading groups in organizations. In P. Goodman & Associates, *Designing effective work groups* (72–119). San Francisco: Jossey-Bass.

HODGETTS, R., & WORTMAN, M., JR. (1975). *Administrative policy: Text and cases in the policy sciences*. New York: John Wiley & Sons.

HOLLAND, T. P. (in progress). *Self-assessment by non-profit boards*.

HOLLAND, T. P., TAYLOR, B. E., & CHAIT, R. P. (1989). Board effectiveness: Identifying and measuring trustee competencies. *Research in Higher Education, 30*(4), 451–469.

HOLLAND, T. P., TAYLOR, B. E., & CHAIT, R. P. (1990). *Survey of governing board effectiveness*. College Park, MD: University of Maryland, National Center for Postsecondary Governance and Finance.

HOULE, C. (1960). *The effective board*. New York: National Board of Young Men's Christian Association.

HOULE, C. (1989). *Governing boards: Their nature and nurture*. San Francisco: Jossey-Bass.

JANIS, I. (1972). *Victims of groupthink*. Boston: Houghton-Mifflin.

KANTER, R. (1983). *The change masters*. New York: Simon & Schuster.

KAUFFMAN, J. (1980). *At the pleasure of the board*. Washington, DC: American Council on Education.

KELLER, G. (1983). *Academic strategy: The management revolution in higher education*. Baltimore: The Johns Hopkins University Press.

KERR, C. (1984). *Presidents make a difference: Strengthening leadership in colleges and universities.* Washington, DC: Association of Governing Boards of Universities and Colleges.

KERR, C., & GADE, M. (1986). *The many lives of academic presidents.* Washington, DC: Association of Governing Boards of Universities and Colleges.

KLEMP, G. & MCCLELLAND, D. (1986). What characterizes intelligent functioning among senior managers? In J. Sternberg & R. Wagner (Eds.), *Practical intelligence: Nature and origins of competence in the every day world* (pp. 31–50). Cambridge, England: Cambridge University Press.

KOTTER, J. & SCHLESINGER, L. Choosing strategies for change. *Harvard Business Review, 57*(2), 106–114.

LAWLER, E. (1973). *Motivation in work organizations.* Monterey, CA: Brooks/Cole.

LEVINSON, H. (1976). Appraisal of what performance? *Harvard Business Review, 54*(4), 30–32, 34, 36, 40, 46, 160.

Lilly Endowment Leadership Education Program (1989). *Depth education training for trustees.* Indianapolis: Lilly Endowment.

LORSCH, J. (1989). *Pawns or potentates: The reality of America's corporate boards.* Boston: Harvard Business School Press.

MASLAND, A. (1985). Organizational culture in the study of higher education. *The Review of Higher Education, 8*(2), 157–168.

MCCALL, M., LOMBARDO, M., & MORRISON, A. (1988). *The lessons of experience: How successful executives develop on the job.* Lexington, MA: Lexington Books.

MEYER, H. (1975). The pay-for-performance dilemma. *Organizational Dynamics,* Winter 1975, 39–50.

MORGAN, G. (1986). *Images of organizations.* Beverly Hills, CA: Sage.

MUELLER, R. (1984). *Behind the boardroom door.* New York: Crown.

NASON, J. (1980). *Presidential assessment: A challenge to college and university leadership.* Washington, DC: Association of Governing Boards of Universities and Colleges.

O'CONNELL, B. (1985). *The board member's book: Making a difference in voluntary organizations.* Washington, DC: The Foundation Center.

O'REILLY, C. (1989). Corporations, culture and commitment: Motivation and social control in organizations. *California Management Review, 31*(4), 285–303.

OUCHI, W. (1981). *Theory z: How American business can meet the Japanese challenge.* Reading, MA: Addison-Wesley.

PATTON, A., & BAKER, J. C. (1987). Why won't directors rock the boat? *Harvard Business Review, 65*(6), 10–18.

PETERS, T., & WATERMAN, R. (1982). *In search of excellence: Lessons from America's best run companies.* New York: Harper & Row.

RICE, R. E., & AUSTIN, A. E. (1988). High faculty morale: What exemplary colleges do right. *Change Magazine, 20*(2), 51–58.

ROSOVSKY, H. (1990). *The university: An owner's manual.* New York: W. W. Norton.

SAVAGE, T. (1982). *The Cheswick process: Seven steps to a more effective board.* Belmont, MA: The Cheswick Center.

SCHEIN, E. (1985). *Organizational culture and leadership.* San Francisco: Jossey-Bass.

SCHON, D. (1983). *The reflective practitioner.* New York: Basic Books.

TAYLOR, B. E. (1987). *Working effectively with trustees: Building cooperative campus leadership* (ASHE-ERIC Research Report No. 2). Washington, DC: Association for the Study of Higher Education.

TAYLOR, B. E. (1988). Results of a survey of board characteristics, policies, and practices. In R. T. Ingram (Ed.), *Making trusteeship work* (pp. 163–182). Washington, DC: Association of Governing Boards of Universities and Colleges.

TIERNEY, W. (1988). Organizational culture in higher education: Defining the essentials. *Journal of Higher Education, 59*(1), 2–21.

WEICK, K. (1983). Managerial thought in the context of action. In S. Srivastva & Associates, *The executive mind: New insights on managerial thought and action* (pp. 221–242). San Francisco: Jossey-Bass.

WHISLER, T. L. (1984). *Rules of the game: Inside the corporate boardroom.* Homewood, IL: Dow Jones-Irwin.

WOOD, M. (1984). Guidelines for an academic affairs committee. In R. P. Chait (Ed.), *Trustee responsibility for academic affairs* (pp. 11–24). Washington, DC: Association of Governing Boards of Universities and Colleges.

WOOD, M. (1985). *Trusteeship in the private college.* Baltimore: The Johns Hopkins University Press.

ZANDER, A., FORWARD, J., & ALBERT, R. (1969). Adaptation of board members to repeated failures or success by their organization. *Organizational Behavior and Human Performance, 4,* 56–76.

ZANDER, A. (1982). *Making groups effective.* San Francisco: Jossey-Bass.

ZWINGLE, J. (1975). *Effective trusteeship.* Washington, DC: Association of Governing Boards of Universities and Colleges.

Index

A

Academic culture, 10–12, 22, 66–67, 77–78
Academic tenure, 10, 11–12, 107
Advisory councils, 57
Agenda development, 105–106
Alderfer, C., 29, 42, 47, 70, 115
Alexander, J., 91
Allison, G., 60n
Anderson, R., 79
Andrews, K., 96
Argyris, C., 88
Ashford, S., 39
Association of Governing Boards (AGB), iv, 7, 13, 21, 28, 29, 38, 58, 90–91, 92n, 107, 113
Austin, A., 93

B

Baker, J., 106, 116–118
Baldridge, J., 10, 22, 77
Behavioral event technique. *See* Critical Incident Technique
Bellah, R., 23
Bennis, W., 96
Bensimon, E., 60
Berliner, D., 67
Bilimoria, D., 4
Birnbaum, R., 60, 69, 78
Blau, P., 114

B

Bolman, L., 59–60
Boyatzis, R., 37
Brainstorming, 74, 126
Brown, S., 89
Butler, L., 17, 106–107
Byrom, F., 34

C

Cameron, K., 4
Carver, J., 13,17
Chaffee, E., 13, 16–17, 62
Chait, R., 4, 10, 22, 27, 38, 43, 104n, 116
Cheswick Center, 17, 38
Clark, B., 19
Cognitive complexity, 59–63, 71–72, 126
Cohen, M., 22, 66, 74, 77
Committee on trusteeship, 38–39, 51, 57, 123
Committees
  evaluating members, 51
  rotating assignments, 36
  structure, 4
Communicating
  within the board, 44–48, 69–73
  with constituencies, 68–69, 81–85;
    president's role, 127–129
  techniques for, 89–93
Conflict management, 85–89
Consent agenda, 106

Cope, R., 100
Critical Incident Technique, 3–4, 37–38

D

Deal, T., 9, 59–60
Dean, J., 56, 120
Delbecq, A., 104, 116
Delphi technique, 73
Devil's advocate, 73
Dill, D., 4
Drucker, P., 7, 8, 12, 17, 115, 132

E

Educating trustees, 26–29, 35–36
Educational Testing Service (ETS), 93
Effectiveness defined, 4–6
    board of trustees, 6
    institutional, 5
Evaluation. *See* Feedback; Self-Assessment

F

Faculty
    autonomy, 10
    communications with board, 82–85
    morale, 93
    role, 22, 79
    service on board committees, 96
    as trustees, 31
Feedback. *See also* Self-Assessment
    external to board, 39–40
    internal to board, 37–39
Fisher, J., 128
Fisher, R., 89
Flanagan, J., 3, 37
Frances, C., 96

G

Gade, M., 116
Gill, S., 104, 116
Gilmore, T., 75
Goodman, P., 56, 120
Governance information system, 106–108, 130
Grooming board leaders, 50–53, 57–58
Group
    dynamics, 44–48

goal setting, 48–50, 55–57
Groupthink, 71
Growth contracts, 57–58

H

Hackman, J., 26, 30
Hodgetts, R., 108
Holland, T., 4
Houle, C., 3, 7, 13, 31

I

Information: *See also* Governance information system
    flow of, 45–46
    search for, 68–69
Institutional history, 22–23

J

Janis, I., 71, 74

K

Kanter, R., 68, 85n
Kauffman, J., 131
Keller, G., 13, 96, 99, 130
Kennedy, A., 9
Kerr, C., 116, 131
Klemp, G., 3
Koch, E., 40
Kotter, J., 86

L

Lawler, E., 31
Levinson, H., 37
Lilly Endowment, 22, 24
Lorsch, J., 31, 116–118
Lynn, R., iv, 22

M

March, J., 22, 66, 74, 77
Masland, A., 9
McCall, M., 32
McClelland, D., 3
Mentors, 28, 55
Meyer, H., 39n
Mission, 12–17
Mistakes, learning from, 32–35

Monitoring
  external environment, 100–101
  institutional climate, 92
  internal environment, 101–103
Morgan, G., 75
Mueller, R., 54, 107

N

Nanus, B., 96
Nason, J., 3, 131
Neumann, A., 60
Nominating committee. *See* Committee on trusteeship

O

O'Connell, B., 3
O'Reilly, C., 56
Organizational culture, 9–10, 21
Orientation, 21–24, 27–28, 55, 89
  advice to newcomers, 65–66, 70–71
  president's role, 119–122
Ouchi, W., 9, 36

P

Patton, A., 106, 116–118
Peters, T., 9, 34
Policy
  board's role, 109–112
  levels of, 108–109
  phases of, 109–110
Presidents
  developing board agenda, 105,
    130–131
  guiding communications with constituencies, 92, 127–129
  need for effective board, 115–118
  providing strategic direction, 104,
    130–131
  role in policy, 109–112
  trustees' perceptions of, 64–65
Public college boards, 7

R

Recruitment and selection, 51, 57,
  119
Research design, 4–6
Retreats, 28–30, 55, 83
  president's role, 122–24
Rice, R., 93

Role playing, 73, 126
Rosovsky, H., 81–82, 99

S

Savage, T., 38, 123
Schein, E., 9–11
Schlesinger, L., 86
Schon, D., 34
Self-assessment by boards, 29–32
  limitation of, 2, 5, 37–39
Shared governance, 22, 78–81, 121
Size of board, 4, 116
  Social relations, 44–45, 53–55,
    124–125
Strategy
  defined, 96
  proactive efforts, 100–103
  setting priorities, 96–99; president's
    role, 130–131
  techniques to focus on, 104–112
Students
  on board committees, 90
  at board orientation, 22
  as trustees, 91

T

Taylor, B., 4, 38, 104n, 116, 119
Tierney, W., 9

U

Umbdenstock, R., 105n

V

Values, 17–21, 23–24, 30

W

Walton, R., 26, 30
Waterman, R., 9, 34
Weick, K., 107n
Whisler, T., 54
Wood, M., 84, 104, 117, 119
Wortman, M., 108

Z

Zander, A., 31, 48, 50, 56–57, 74
Zwingle, J., 3